Room to Fly

The publisher gratefully
acknowledges the generous
contribution to this book
provided by The General
Endowment Fund of the
Associates of the University
of California Press.

Room to Fly

A Transcultural Memoir

Danny, Lisa, Julie &

Matthew —

much love,

Padma

PADMA HEJMADI

University of California Press

Berkeley Los Angeles London

University of California Press
Berkeley and Los Angeles, California

University of California Press, Ltd.
London, England

Library of Congress
Cataloging-in-Publication Data
Hejmadi, Padma.
Room to fly: a transcultural memoir /
Padma Hejmadi.
p. cm.
ISBN 0-520-21506-0 (alk. paper)
1. Hejmadi, Padma—Journeys.
2. Women authors, Indic—20th
century Biography. 3. East Indians—
Foreign countries—Biography.
4. Women—India—Biography.
5. Voyages and travels. 6. Cultural
relations. 7. Spiritual life.
PR9499.3.P4 Z47 1999
828—dc21
[B]   99-19034

Printed in the United States of America
9 8 7 6 5 4 3 2 1

To Padma from her godma

The Japanese school of Sumi painting says:
if you depict a bird, give it space to fly.

Contents

Prologue

Over the years and across the cultures and continents of my life, I have
sought to carve a Sumi space and define its elements—in illness and
health, in peace or trouble, in solitude, in intimacies, in the functional
schizophrenia that can chop up a day not only into commitments, obli-
gations, and the scramble for a livelihood, but also what a friend calls
"the intricate slaughter of life." And I think of the many who struggle
as I do, against far more stringent circumstances, to claim this spatial
birthright.

Calling it a combination of physical, psychological and emotional
space may be justified, but that's too easy, too categorical. For this area
includes a certain ecology of the spirit. After all, in giving the bird space
you are not giving it *something*, you are giving it *nothing*—except its

due: an expression of what is already its own, which is the need and ability to fly. That is it, finally. The honoring, the recognition of an entity in its implicit and life-giving habitat: its survival, our survival.

"Sumi spaces," then, in allowing room to fly, have to be both large enough and small enough to take in various entities and expressions of survival. Such spaces—containing, among other things, language as well as silence, stillness as well as movement—inevitably exist across diverse landscapes, summoning the architecture as well as the ambience of a place, the way people move and sit and walk on their land, the way they shape its spaces, the way it shapes theirs.

I must cross the few cultures and continents I have partially glimpsed, cross geography and time too, to chart some quintessential spaces and attest to this verticality of travel (those inner dimensions scaled even when you are standing still): pinpointing the place, within and without, where an insight was glimpsed, though it may have been assimilated only later. Being in the moment utterly, yes—eat an apple when you eat an apple, as Zen phraseology might have it—but then trying also to move on from there as mindfully and scrupulously as possible, bringing any intellectual or imaginative arabesques back to the authentic human experience where they belong.

It is, after all, that old process which Katherine Mansfield once described as "going out and looking at a tree and coming back *plus* the tree."

Glorious Illiteracy

Tirunelveli

At age five, in this small town in the very far south of India, I refuse to be made literate. Learning to read and write means learning to read and write in English, and now that the time has come for me to go to school, my great-aunt—peppery, fiercely nationalistic—says: "So? The British will leave shortly and we'll be independent. But you? You'll still be a slave. You will learn their language and have them on your tongue forever."

So on the first day of school I mount my revolution and run away, and they have a rule thereafter that the gates should be kept shut.

That evening we are walking down the path from the house to the river, my mother and I, and I yell: I won't go to school. I won't be a slave. I won't, I won't. First my mother says "Nonsense," as we pause to examine the filaments of a cobweb on the jackfruit tree. "How can learning make you a slave? At most, it tells you how other people live with their language the way we do with ours. Tools for the mind, like clothes for the body, you see?"

I won't see and I won't look at the cobweb and I won't go to school and I keep yelling it all out at the top of my voice until we come to a dead stop. Amma kneels down right there on the path so that our eyes can meet on the same level. "Look," she says. "Learning is not a bitter pill for you to swallow, making faces. It is an honor, a gift. The day you come to me with a paper and pencil and say, 'I want to learn how to read and write,' you shall. Not until then. You don't deserve it." If you are stubborn with Amma, she is stubborn right back at you; but even when she isn't on your side, somehow she is.

We keep our pact. I begin two years of glorious illiteracy—a period, I subsequently realize, of which I have almost total recall: for the world around me is my only book. I learn about herbs and herbal medicine, plant myths, river myths, thievery, stories about the guardian demiurges round about. Their life-size sculptures stand at the threshold to each village, facing north, whence come all calamities.

Sudalaimadan is the most powerful. He has a high hat like a Christian archbishop, a fierce black moustache, bulging eyes; and he brandishes a sword with his right hand while his left rests on a murderous club, painted magenta. He can take any form he wishes . . . an elephant; a man on a white horse, dressed in coat and jodhpurs; a bull trampling the crops; a pig; a bear. If you hear an unexplained scream in the middle of the night, it is Sudalaimadan calling his brother Isakki to come catapulting out of the underworld: HELP! SOMETHING HAS HAPPENED! And if you hear equally unexplained weeping at midday, don't go anywhere near, don't. It is Isakki, disguised as a lovely sixteen-year-old to snare passersby as a snack for lunch.

There is also the pei (ghost) of an Englishman who died in battle and needs to be given brandy, a cigar, a Western loaf of bread, and a pair of leather boots hung from a branch. You have to accommodate their quirks. In the southwest corner of a nearby Hindu temple lives a Muslim pei. Why he chooses that habitat, nobody knows. What he wants, everybody knows. Ganja: pot. Leave him a bit every night and he'll leave you alone.

"That's the trouble," I quaver to Ramu, the gardener. "There are so many. How am I to know what each one wants?"

"Simple," says Ramu. "Just as you'd be careful with snakes. You don't be too curious, or cross them, and they won't be too curious, or cross you."

"But suppose I walk over one and don't even know it's there?"

"Simple," he says again. "Keep a bunch of neem twigs with you. You can ward them all off with that."

Thereafter I carry neem twigs with me wherever I go, sleep with some under my pillow at night, and (in situations that demand circumspection) secretly tuck a few leaves into the elastic of my knickers, until a red ant crawls out from among those leaves and bites my belly.

Ramu it is who also knows about herbs. He has planned a medicinal garden—"Right there, beyond the neem tree." He points to the open space south of the house and makes a square shape with his hands.

"So close to the neem?"

"Not so close, just close enough. SHE lives there."

"Who?"

"Shitala. The cool one. Goddess of the pox. Seated on a swing."

From where we stand, the neem tree looks rather cloudy in the distance, but up close the leaves are fretted nervous and delicate, and shapes move among them.

"Have you seen her?"

Ramu spits accurately into the jasmine bush. "What is there to see? If anyone is sick with the pox and you break off even a small branch and fan the invalid—*then* you'll see. When they get better, if you put neem leaves into the water for the first bath—*then* you'll see."

He squats down and starts to weed the jasmine bush, slapping my hand away when I try to help. "You don't know anything. This is *my* work."

So I find a blade of grass to chew and squat by him. "Who told you all this?"

"The priest in our village. Not like the others, mumbling mantras all the time. *He* grew his herbs right by the temple courtyard. He could heal. People came from everywhere."

"He had power?" I ask, awed.

"Nah," Ramu says scornfully. "Not power. Just plants." Reaching up, he strokes the jasmine leaves with his muddy fingers. He smells of that mud, and his sweat, and a kind of knowing, very sure of itself. "The priest told me you should always plant tulasi* in the center, to keep evil away: never pluck the leaves on a Thursday or a Saturday; never boil them, that will torment the soul of the plant. He said"—Ramu struggles, trying to twist his tongue around the Sanskrit words to get them right— "He said: tulasi-tulana-nasti, ataeva-tulasi. . . . It means, nothing can equal the goodness of the tulasi." For a moment the priest speaks solemnly from his mouth. Then Ramu returns to his daily voice, matter-

---

* Tulasi: *Ocimum sanctum,* sacred basil.

4

of-fact. "That is what I will plant first in my garden." He makes the square shape with his hands once more, and jabs it in the middle.

"What else?"

"Datura."

"Datura!" Not those huge trumpet-shaped white flowers that hang face downward, as if ashamed of their own poison!

"Yes," Ramu says, surer than ever. "The thing with poison: if you can see it to tell it, you can sometimes use it. But I wouldn't use the blossoms anyway, only the leaves. Spread them over a swelling of the joints, bind them down with a wet cloth. . . ." When he pauses, a green damp seeps through the bandage. "And nellikai. You think it's just like a plain old gooseberry? Nah. Purifies the blood. Oh, and senna for constipation." He pats his stomach; he weeds some more; I chew my grass-blade down to its end. The river spangles through the trees; the sun is hot.

"You look at some plants. . . ." At first he seems to be talking to himself. "And you think oh yes, very nice, very pretty, that's all. Ole-anders. Do you know"—his turbaned head comes down close—"their roots, ground up, can cure skin disease? You don't know. See? What did I tell you? You don't know anything."

Satisfied, he pulls out another weed, and I find another grass-blade to chew, and think about oleanders.

"Some," Ramu continues, "you don't even have to plant. They grow by themselves. Like neglu-mulloo."

Who would ever want to plant neglu-mulloo, I wonder to myself. They are all over the wild grounds behind the house. Round, spiked thorns, prickly whichever way you turn them, so that they stick to your clothes and skin and have to be pried painfully loose, one by one.

"Make a tea with them," Ramu advises me. "Just boil in hot water.

Drink it if you have trouble peeing. And those yellow flowers by the back gate. . . ."

I remember the old book my father showed me from his library, with engraved illustrations and Latin names I can't read, though I love the sound of them. "Yes. Father calls it *Cassia . . . Cassia . . .*" my turn to struggle now, *"Cassia auriculata."*

"I don't know about all that," Ramu waves a dismissing hand. "All I know is, keep those flowers in a bowl of water to bathe your eyes whenever they get sticky and scratchy with pus."

I blink. The house, the garden, the river, disappear. My eyelids stick, and then unstick, healed.

"And see over there?" You can easily miss the small round leaves he's pointing at, except for their stench. But this time I know better than to offer my father's name for it, which is *Ruta graveolens*. Syllable by syllable I've learned it again for love of its weird sound. "Wards off snakes. And the leaves are just the thing for certain kinds of snake bites. Also certain kinds of fits." Suddenly he is shaking all over and falls back on the grass, writhing and flailing about. Then he opens one eye. "That is, if the stink of those leaves in the first place isn't enough to cure you before you start anything. But don't tell anybody."

I haven't. Not until now.

And there is the river. All the dry season long, it is just a thread of silver, winding through the vast white sand-bed where washermen spread out their clothes to dry in the sun. But during the monsoons it swirls full and tempestuous, drowning trickle and sand-bed alike as it swells and tosses from bank to bank, the exact color of very milky tea. . . . At the marriage of Shiva and Parvathi on holy Mount Kailash, the presence of all the other gods who gathered at the wedding tilted the earth so perilously that the great sage Agastya had to be sent south to balance it again with the weight of his learning and goodness. When he left, he took with him a handful of pink lotuses from the wedding garland; and when he saw how parched the south had become, he flung down the petals, and they turned into a river, and gave it both its color and its name: Tambaraparni, which can mean either Copper Water, or River of Red Leaves.

And there are the ancient burial urns north of the town. Scholars keep coming down from the universities, and the townspeople try to tell them: "Listen, these ancient people: the older they grew the more mischievous they became; and the more mischievous they became, the more they shrank. Until at last they grew so small and everyone else was in such a rage that they *stuffed* the little creatures into the urns." But the scholars won't listen. They don't know that if you don't watch out, you can shrink.

And there is the house. Our house only for as long as my father is posted to this district. Most visitors round their eyes in astonishment at its sheer size, slewing their heads from side to side to take in the whole long sweep of its pillared verandahs—which I bicycle up and down on rainy days—or supporting their necks with their hands as they crane back to take in its height, gasping: "Ooh, like a palace."

But of course it isn't a palace. It is, my aunt Rekha says, "just a dumbfoundingly huge and decrepit old house built in the early days of the East India Company." She is studying to be an architect and has come to spend her holidays with us. Instead of rounding her eyes, she narrows them—"to measure the perspectives, you ignorant child"—and walks all over, every inch, aligning corners, tapping walls, and inspecting the great old half-shuttered doors, not one of whose latches works.

"Aren't you afraid to live in a house where you can't lock a single door?" others ask us.

Such questions never enter *her* head. "Look at the height of that ceiling," is what she says. "Each floor two stories high, at least. They must have used the downstairs as godowns—to store grain in times of famine, perhaps, or as warehouses in which to cram the evidence of their nefarious trade." Her words are long (even as I translate them now) whenever she talks about the house: it is big enough to hold them.

Together we decide we must invent a special festival to honor it, a festival unlike all the others that measure out the year, festivals handed down by everybody else to honor everything else. "Because *this* is worth its own celebration," my aunt says. "STURDY. They had terrible floods here during the last century. I looked it up in the District Gazetteer of that time. The bridge across the river was safe. The British finally built it in 1833 and an elephant was the first to walk across. So it was strong enough . . . and high enough, that's the main thing. But here the whole ground floor was under water. Everyone fled upstairs and stayed there, marooned but safe, until they were rescued. And the house withstood it all—floods, ravages, repairs."

The water must have been muddy during the floods, but I see it clear and sunlit, rippling between the white pillars, and the old house standing strong and still.

"And don't forget," my aunt Rekha reminds me, "If you don't celebrate it, someone else will, in their own different way. One of these days, this place will be protected under the National Monuments Act, and then nobody else will ever live in it again."

It is as if we are all slipping away with the water as it recedes; you have to hurry and catch hold.

"Why?"

"Because it's historical, that's why. There's supposed to be a secret passage somewhere. I haven't found it yet, though God knows I've tapped the walls loud and long enough. Some say the English general hid here while escaping the Nawab of Arcot's men. Or maybe *they* were escaping from *him*, who knows? It was all so long ago." She yawns and looks sleepy. "Anyway, when you go to school and start learning about the causes and effects of the Carnatic Wars, remember you played with history in this house."

She knows well enough I won't go to school, but we ignore that for the moment. "What about the festival? How should we celebrate it?"

"Choose a day," my aunt says. "Choose a way. Think about it." She rumples my head and walks off, humming a film song.

But the house is never the same again. Now the stairs thunder with invisible footsteps; ranks of sweating soldiers crowd the verandahs; and outside, the garden loses its green and grows ragged beneath the trampling of horses' hooves.

And there are other nights when it all fades, and the moonlight washes through where once the water must have, and the old house stands strong and still, waiting for a festival I cannot name.

There is so much to hold, how can you pick a single way?

And then there are the Maravas. An old tribe of thieves belonging to the district from way back. Very proud of their profession and respected for their skill, until years and years ago the English passed the Criminal Tribes Act and called them (I am to discover even more years later)

K.D.'s, short for Known Depredators. After this, earning their livelihood became harder and harder for the Maravas. But they move with the times. Over the past few decades, instead of having the police go around and check on them in their houses, they have offered courteously to come and sleep in front of the district jail during the dry season—nice and fresh and open there, right under the eye of authority. Besides, with so many of them packed together, who can notice on a moonless night if one or two are missing? After all, by morning they are back with the rest, sleeping there as good as gold.

Their instruction comes into my life after the festival for Saraswathi, goddess of learning and skill and the arts. She is titular deity to us Saraswath Brahmans, though everybody shares in her worship on this day. Mohammed, who sometimes drives the car, doesn't let his being a Muslim stop him from celebrating the instrument of *his* skill. He festoons its hood with garlands of marigolds, puts a red dot of kumkum between the headlights, and stands back with his head on one side to admire the effect. "Pretty as a woman," he says. Early morning our household shrine is cleaned and washed and decorated with flowers, and a bare place is made beneath Saraswathi's silk portrait for all the instruments and implements to be especially blessed by her. My mother's violin and veena are brought there; my sister's school books; Ramu's gardening tools; pots and ladles from the cook; and I am dutifully laying out the ankle bells I wear while dancing when we discover—in the middle of the array of offerings—a jimmy and a picklock.

It turns out then that a Marava is in the compound—not *doing* anything, just resting, while he brings a message for a cousin's friend who lives in the buildings by the south gate. There is a small rise like a hillock here, from where you can see the house, the wild thorn-ridden grounds behind it, the garden before it, and the river beyond. Here on the hillock the Marava sits endlessly cleaning his teeth with a neem twig. My sister (who, when she was three, had thought that a thief was a perfectly round house with one door and two windows) is too busy now with older preoccupations, so I go alone to have a chat with him.

He is dressed like anyone else in a dhothi and a shirt, but his head is shaven bare except for a topknot of long straight black hair. Every now and then he unties it, shakes it out, slaps it into the air once, twice, thrice, then takes a wooden comb from his pocket to streamline it carefully through before retying the knot again. "Nothing much happening now," he complains, low and gloomy. "But in the old days, in my grandfather's days, in my father's even—ah, what thievery!"

It is a long story, the way it used to happen, the way he tells it now, with many pauses to shift the neem twig from one cheek to the other and stare off into the distance.

Every expedition in those glorious days really begins on the night before, with the raiding party praying to Sudalaimadan and laying a crowbar at his feet to promise that any further offerings will be strictly in proportion to the haul. Always there are omens before, during, and after the ceremony. Chirp of lizard to the left, hoot of an owl, cat running across from left to right, all mean disaster: postpone the raid. When they do set out, each one takes a particular name: Hatchet or Knife or Club. . . . Some carry stones at their waists. Once a hole has been bored in the house under attack, or a window forced open, a stone is dropped in to see if the clatter will awaken anybody. If all is still, the thinnest— Knife—wriggles through first and lets the others in.

"Not so now," the Marava repeats. "Not so easy . . ." and goes off into another of his long silences, from which he suddenly emerges more cheerful. "Except sometimes. Of course nobody can carry stones and hatchets now, with them watching us all the time. But sometimes you don't need any of that. Sometimes . . ." his voice drops, "all you need is a single strand from a broom."

"A single—?" I am agog.

"Yes." For the first time he looks at me, weighing me. Perhaps I am too young and riveted an audience to be dangerous, so he tells me that too. "You know how a traveller will always put whatever is most valuable to him under his pillow at night, stupid fellow, and then put his stupid head directly on top of it? Well—just wait until he is asleep, then take your strand of broomstick and tickle his ear. *Very* lightly, like a mosquito. He'll brush it off . . . or slap it away . . . or mumble . . . maybe even show signs of waking up. Then you stay quiet until he goes back to sleep before you start again. Brush—slap—scratch—mumble . . . and he'll turn over. So you slip your hand exactly under where he's just removed his head, and remove what *you* want. That's all there is to it." He sounds every bit as sure as Ramu.

After his departure—and nobody has missed so much as a handful of grain—my worldly education comes to an abrupt and deadly dull stop. The rains set in earlier than usual, falling in dreary ropes straight down from the sky and holding you in like a net. Dampness, stickiness, nothing to do. My sister is in school, my father away most of the time in the low-lying districts where, if you don't work hard enough soon enough, checking on irrigation canals, strengthening tank bunds and sandbagging water boundaries, there is always a danger of floods. When he is home, he is hardly to be seen. People keep coming around to the southern, "official" end of the house. Men with file folders and briefcases mount the shallow steps to the octagonal Meeting Room.

Once I sneak past Nabbi, the red-uniformed attendant outside, and get down on my stomach to peer beneath the swinging half-doors, and count twenty pairs of feet around the conference table. Of them all, my father's are the most recognizable, by their impatient tapping if the speeches go on too long. I tap my fingers in time, in sympathy.

"That's his way," a whisper sounds above, guessing what I'm doing.

Nabbi is not only undisturbed at finding me flat on the floor there, he is even in the mood for a chat. We go to the far end of the verandah, where you are out of earshot if you speak softly. "Other people talk much and do little, he talks little and does much. Look at what happened with the man-eating tiger."

The moment Nabbi names a wild animal, it comes alive in front of you. Maybe because he looks rather like a lion himself, with his burly shoulders and tawny eyes and beard like a mane, dyed red after his pilgrimage to Mecca. The pilgrimage has made him a Haji and gives him authority when he speaks. "I've worked here many years, seen many heads of the district come and go. None like him."

"What happened about the man-eater?"

"It was marauding an area about thirty miles from here. Near a village trapped between the river and the jungle, so the people had no place to run. First their livestock was carried off, then their children. Nobody was safe. So they complained to the government. Anyone else might have sat down and written a hundred and one reports. Not he. He just went out and got a gun and shot it. Had to be done, so he did it. That's all." And Nabbi pads off.

That's all, he says. *That's all there is to it,* says the Marava. *Simple,* says Ramu. Except once. *Think about it,* says my aunt Rekha. And the rain goes on and on, and your footsteps echo before and behind you as you walk against the endless drumming. Lamps have to be lit all day; the greyness turns them yellow and too dim to cast their usual shimmer on the floors. Outside, though the bamboo screens have been lowered between the pillars, gusts of spattering raindrops keep the verandahs skidding wet. This gives my great-aunt a pain in her joints and she takes either to bed or to quarrelling, refusing to speak to anyone for days on end. Only Amma remains the same, moving quick and light through the huge old rooms, with the household keys jingling at her waist, or sitting down in the evenings to play her veena or to read.

Leaning over her shoulder, I see the book open on her lap. It has an illustration drawn in swift flying black lines: people in a room, with rain outside the window. The women have foreign clothes, short hair and bare legs. But reading cannot be so different after all, if it rains inside books as well as out. There might even be floods in them then, and broomsticks, and villages, and fear of man-eaters, and pilgrims like Nabbi with beards dyed red.

"What are those people doing? What does it say?"

Amma looks up and smiles. "Are you asking me, or do you want to know for yourself?" Her question goes on and on into the dripping dusk.

There's a table wedged against the wall. Its square top, inlaid with patterned shell and bone and ebony, opens on hinges like a lid; and you look inside for strings and pins and clips and pencils and erasers and pads of paper. I tear off a sheet, find a stub of a red pencil, and return to her. "For myself. I want to read and write."

After this it is magic. Also, in other ways, no different. Perhaps I haven't become a slave yet. Small ls are simple and straight as legs. Capital P is Ramu with his hand to his turban, thinking about herbs. Y is Nabbi facing Mecca with both arms raised in prayer. And when these and the other letters are pulled together into words, those words can be punched and pummelled and shifted and shaped like clay into their exact place next to each other, until at last you can say what you see: just *so*.

Soon there are numbers. 1 is so skinny because he hates to eat. His parents keep prodding him: eat, eat; but no, he won't. 2 is so curly and graceful because she is a dancer. 3, 6, and 9 are friends, but 5 and 7 can't stand one another because they are so angular that their bones bump if you put them together. If I get a sum whose answer is 57, quickly quickly I rub it out and write 56 instead.

"Why do you *do* that?" Amma asks, exasperated but willing as usual to listen.

"They'll fight. Their elbows will get in the way and they'll fight. What else can I do?"

Delhi

"Nothing, clearly." My mother answers that question of more than twenty years ago. "I'm not surprised that the spaces of your learning have been so crammed ever since." We are talking together, she and I, in the sunlight of a northern winter, about the interplay of imagination and intelligence—in living, and in certain kinds of learning, whether you are literate or not.

"Like Phulo," she reminds me.

Phulo is the sister-in-law of the farmer who sells water-buffalo milk to our neighborhood. She is a widow, crippled and illiterate; she has inherited some land and livestock; and the men in her in-laws' family are planning to sell her—*sell* her—to a scoundrel of a neighboring landlord so that they can weasel some joint property out of the transaction.

Phulo, that living property, comes desperately to my mother for help, as those in trouble do. "I have to get out of there before they take me away. But I have to think about my son also. What am I to do? Where can I go? Where can I get a job that will give me an excuse to leave the farm at once?"

For over a year, my great-aunt's cardiac asthma has been getting worse. A matter of time, they say. A matter of slowly watching her die. We take turns nursing, but Amma has done most of it; and the nights have asserted their cost, since the days don't lessen their full measure of other demands and duties. So Phulo arrives, to keep the night-watch. And stays on with the family thereafter, in one capacity or another. When Americans reach the moon, my gentle aunt asks: "How would you feel about going there?" Phulo says, indefatigable, "If you go, I go. Just get me the bus ticket."

But on that first night of her arrival, Amma and I go into the sick-room around midnight to see how she is managing. Only one small night light burns. The row of medicine bottles casts monstrous shadows on the wall. As we enter, we see her gently moving my great-aunt's arm, and then her leg.

I whisper: "What are you doing?"

She whispers back: "When people have been ill for so long that they haven't the strength to move a limb, we must move it for them. Or else they get sores where they lie. This is how we look after our cattle."

We stand there, half-smiling at that, despite our anxiety and our book-learning, while it is Phulo, again, who notices what the invalid can't ask for. "See? Her lips are dry now, she needs water . . ." holding a spoonful against my great-aunt's mouth. Some dribbles, some she drinks.

Now in the winter sunlight, Amma and I remember that. Not to discount literacy or sentimentalize its lack, but honoring Phulo's ability to anticipate the wordless—that keen applying of empathy and observation to life.

"Maybe that's why I took a chance on letting you go illiterate," Amma smiles at me, with me. "Hoping some of that wisdom might rub off on you."

"Actually, in Tirunelveli literacy made no difference. Wonderful of you not to make me go to school until we moved to Madras—only then did I realize it was the Thin End Of The Wedge."

Which, said suddenly and portentously in English, makes us both laugh. But we agree that in my encounters later with a women's college in Delhi as earlier with the middle schools of Madras, literacy—in the cramped or rigid way it is disseminated—often *is* a slavery, though perhaps not quite as my great-aunt envisioned it.

Still, for me as for others, it also provides a peculiar and only freedom, the freedom at least to make my own stubborn world, writing; knowing full well that what I'm doing is still learning—an apprenticeship which may never stop being an apprenticeship; so that in Madras I feed my finished pages to a hot-water boiler we derivatively call Ophelia because it's quite mad. It stands on three legs in the backyard, smokes foully, and has a door at the bottom that you open to shove in the fuel—wood, coal, paper. Pages. My burnt offerings.

Ophelia is tangible, but there are other intangibles that will not be confined to the disciplines within, which inevitably have to reckon, as we all do, with the world outside.

Referring to this, Amma muses: "Right from the beginning you've imposed so many inner restrictions on yourself. And inner restrictions, whether they're self-imposed or beyond one's control, must make external restrictions—particularly when they make no sense—*unbearable*."

More years later, living in a country where "literacy" is more prevalent, and learning about the anguish of dyslexics, I want them all to meet her.

My mother. My mother. As someone said: just let them try to cut *this* umbilical cord. Just let them try.

Wet Pavements

New York

On a rainy evening here, I wonder what it is like to be born to a single language. To speak, work and live within the scope of this one service-able tongue, launching into others largely in the spirit of an excursion or a specialty—for pleasure perhaps? Curiosity? Scholarship? Otherwise to accept the polyglot world as just another geographical fact, not the ingrained and inchoate substance of whatever you eat or dream or once slid under, as a child.

Maybe rainy evenings evoke conjectures of this sort because they muffle the insistence of your immediate surroundings. Wet pavements look like wet pavements all the world over; it is easier then to bring together the different languages you inhabit, for their differences seem to stand equal beneath the anonymous rain. Differences of all kinds.

Physical differences, as in a certain sound your ear gets used to, or a certain gesture that impels your hand. Mental differences, whether in your proficiency or in your association of ideas: those subtler and more subjective contours of knowledge that come from living every day with another language.

As an example there is my own dubious Spanish, which appears and disappears depending upon the context. It was picked up piecemeal (a smattering in a classroom, a bit more from Spanish-speaking friends) simply by learning to place everything from a political opinion to a favorite poem to the high, exasperated edge of family quarrels in it. Always loved, always easy to pronounce, it brings a pause and a rhythm and an extravagance even easier to assimilate. So though I still can't summon the language at will, it remains an irreplaceable part of my consciousness, and to that extent I "know" it.

Obviously this kind of knowledge could never be allowed by any self-respecting dictionary definition. According to Webster, a bilingual person uses "two languages habitually and with a control like that of a native speaker." By extension, then, a multilingual person should be similarly versed in several languages. Yet the human brain, we are told, is incapable of handling more than two or three languages with any degree of perfection. Clearly there are exceptions to this rule: a linguist, for one, or a professional interpreter. However, even interpreters at the United Nations—whose building stands there, several rainy streets across this city—are required to know no more than three official languages, only one of which they translate into. No matter how many other languages they might wield, it is this "active" one of which they must have absolute command. And as for scholarly linguists, they usually deal with what one expert calls a "rather limited set of notions." To be "at home" in another language, he says, is much harder, for "knowing two languages perfectly means, among other things, remembering two words or phrases for every little detail of life." That in turn becomes a question of emphasis rather than efficiency, for often, depending on the bilingual person's environment or personal predilection, one of his or her languages gains ascendancy while the other correspondingly lapses.

Me, I can't equate my languages at all. Put them side by side and they promptly stand in a snaggle-toothed row, refusing to be bound by the same rule. One has become a tool, another its possible alternative, a third is reduced to an instinct, the fourth hovers in my head like a tantalizing tune just out of reach, the fifth is background to the whole lot, and so on. Growing up in India you become a polyglot by osmosis. Or if you don't, you should. At the last count we had fifteen major languages (each with a script and centuries-old literature of its own), eight hundred dialects and one thousand six hundred fifty-four mother tongues. A resigned old proverb says, "Language changes every fifteen miles," which about sums up the ensuing chaos. To complicate matters further, I come from a peripatetic family. We therefore needed a working knowledge of several Indian languages at a time as we moved from state to state; and when, as an adult, I went to study, work, travel and live abroad for considerable periods, I had to reckon with international languages as well.

Being polylingual in such situations is finally neither an accomplishment nor even the muddle-headed necessity it started out as. It so prisms, refracts certain perceptions that you are afflicted with a kind of lifelong interior astigmatism. You undergo sudden baffling transpositions within yourself, especially in your emotional responses to certain words or phrases. You witness somersaults of meaning across the whole changing focus of language, living and location. (One dialect I know puns "soap" with "husband.") At other times you see no collateral concept in one language to express what is clear to you in another—not from any lack in your own proficiency but because of a lack in the language itself: an absence of vocabulary and thought alike, where there is no cultural raison d'être for the term, no collective idea or experience to warrant a particular word. (The first missionaries who sailed to the Andaman Islands, all rarin' to convert the heathen, found to their stupefaction that the local inhabitants had no word for God.) Often you must also contend with a layered, superimposed vision that gives you a different perspective on the same word in different cultural contexts.

"Green," for instance: ecologically endangered in all languages across the earth. In my mother tongue, Konkani, the word for me is particularly imbued with the intense, life-giving green of rice fields, filling the belly and staving off death. In English it has seasonal implications (summer leaves), or overtones of finance (a greenback) or ineptitude (a greenhorn; in the Indian languages I know, novices aren't green, merely unripe). And after Lorca's "verde que te quiero verde," the Spanish "green" is unrivaled—even by Andrew Marvell's "green thought in a green shade." Translating snatches of poetry in your head, like translating slang or proverbs, can be disastrous, and not only because of what every translator knows: that words which mean the same don't *feel* the same. (One terrible translation of Neruda says "belly button" for "navel" and kills the poem.) Tonight I drive myself crazy trying to render into Hindi the woman so exquisitely wrought that even her body thought. In Hindi she isn't; it doesn't.

Limbos lie between languages. Textures of hiatus. Why does a nursery superstition like "things happen in threes" never make you quail as does the far more ominous "jamais deux sans trois"? And what incomparable grace does the simplest Greek *kalimera* have that our own greetings never quite match? Not even when *namasté* means "I honor the light within you"? The thrill of the exotic is only part of it.

After all, there are gaps enough even in the connotations of a single word within a single language. Bertrand Russell, speaking of social and individual knowledge, remarks on how "rain" has an entirely different meaning for a child in the tropics as against a child in a temperate climate. For me, straddling both worlds, this applies in another way. "Rain" in my dialect resounds with the immediate fury of a monsoon, whereas in English it is much more malleable, accommodating everything from a drizzle to a downpour.

As long as experience molds vocabulary, and both occur across radically differing cultures, there can be no hard and fast formula. A rule of thumb in one language becomes a non sequitur in another. In one language you can run into yourself coming back. In another, there's no such thing. Courtesies grow flexible: you discover how politely you can be rude in Urdu. Conversely, insolence in the Eastern world becomes candor in the West, leaving you to applaud directness in the very breath that you deplore it.

Even the quality of the imagination shifts. When R. L. Stevenson describes his wife wondering herself crazy over the human eyebrow, it's perfectly obvious that she wondered in English. In at least three other languages I can think of, the process would have been not only heavy-handed but heavy-footed, like wading in glue.

Then, before you know it, metaphors and imprecations have changed places. If an owl, so proudly stamped on an Athenian coin, is guaranteed wise in English, in Hindi it is the ultimate epithet for stupidity.

Earlier this afternoon a friend stopped by for a visit, and I maundered on to her much as I have here, and about much the same things. We agreed that being caught between words and languages was in any case

23

as human a predicament as being caught between emotions or principles; then we drifted off into a companionable quiet, listening to the rain thrumming on the windowpanes and peering out into a light as splintered as my languages.

Now she has left. In my mind I trace her route home through the wet streets, and pause once more at the lingual spaces contained in the U.N. Building. Its structure expands and diminishes. It becomes a pebble thrown into a pool—ripples widening in implication beyond the immediate expertise of its interpreters to the very bounds of survival inherent in the relationship between a people and their language, past all the convulsions of history, politics, emigration and exile.

Mere expatriates or cross-cultural itinerants have it much easier. We can afford our idiosyncracies.

Chennai

What does it mean to inherit a language without a script?

I must return to my girlhood for this one, and to my cousin Premi's wedding in a square grey house in what was the far rural edge of this South Indian city then known as Madras. Yet the mother tongue itself retains a muscularity of the present tense: still flexible, though it won't be budged from that beginning, the moment and place that first brought an awareness of our oral tradition.

The front door has been auspiciously festooned with mango leaves, the dry delicate line of them lifting in the wind. Rice fields stretch all around, punctuated by the sudden scatter-white of paddybirds' wings against that life-giving green. Rows of palmyras stalk stiffly off toward the canal and the town beyond. Inside, the house smells of sandalwood and crushed silk, and four generations are flung pell-mell together: mothers tending their babies in the long room upstairs; aunts and great-aunts supervising in the kitchen over the irate explosions of the cook; cousins running out at the last minute to fetch something or other the priest forgot; great-uncles ranged on the front verandah, flapping their newspapers over politics like elderly moths; every now and then the whole place having to be turned upside down, as when someone loses a ring or a necklace (eventually found in the soap dish, where the owner put it while taking a bath); everybody in a continual bustle of preparation ... *gadbadi*, we call it.

And suddenly, given the relative obscurity of our dialect, Konkani, and the minuteness of our linguistic community dispersed across the subcontinent (at that point probably sixty thousand out of 400 million), I am astounded that all of us in this house should speak the same language, share the same crazy-quilt of its heritage.

Given our usual blur between hearsay and history, Konkani perhaps began as a lost language spoken by our ancestors in Kashmir when they lived well before the Christian era on the banks of the equally lost river Saraswathi. (We are still called Saraswaths, though, after the river and its goddess Saraswathi, who fosters learning and the arts.) From Kashmir and contiguous areas of the north, the ancestors are thought to have migrated south in different batches—maybe when the Huns overran parts of the north in the fifth century C.E.; and again during and after 1000 C.E., as Muslim invaders came pouring through the Himalayan passes, converting the local populace on the pain of death. Whereupon some died, some converted, some lay low, and some fled. Our latest lot of ancestors apparently fled, taking a century or more over their journey south.

During this period they, like their predecessors, seem to have indulged in a kind of linguistic kleptomania, picking up shreds and tag-ends of other languages along the way. What mixture were they speaking when they reached the west coast of southern India and either built or encountered the earliest ancestral stone temple built by the sea near Goa? Nobody knows. Settlers old and new had to flee again when the Portuguese, who colonized Goa, imported the Inquisition after 1492. Most families were killed, burned and mutilated during the auto-da-fé. Some escaped inland, carrying gods to safekeeping in jungles: to temples disguised as houses, to houses disguised as farms. (*Only animals here, please, only animals. . . . Whiskers twitch. An ear flaps down in the dark.*) Other survivors, less encumbered, went even farther down the west coast, trekking through forests or going by sea, and eventually settling in villages around the port of Mangalore.

To this day, many of us remain linked by our surnames to these old habitats, for when the clans resided for a time in a particular village, they simply took its name as their own. The bride's brother, who specializes in apocryphal tales, claims that their original village had two huts. The monsoons came and blew one down, so now there's one hut left. This says something, at any rate, about the relative sparseness of later generations who have since moved away to live in other parts of the country.

But wherever we may be across the subcontinent, we still tend to be accused with monotonous regularity of being southern by northerners and northern by southerners—partly because of our predilections (in general we eat southern food and like northern music) but mainly because of our language, which continues to deploy original root-words from both the Aryan north and the Dravidian south, agglutinates included: prepositions, postpositions and all. We are defined by it, this cockeyed dialect I love, now sounding through the house.

I have to call it dialect for want of a better word. Unlike English dialects, most of which remain recognizably English and scarcely modify the standard tongue, Konkani is a distinct language in itself. Today it is spoken with extraordinary variations up and down what is indeed now called the Konkan Coast—larded with Bombay's Marathi at its northern end, Kerala's Malayalam at its southern end, and vestiges of Portuguese in between, around Goa. (Goa has been able to use the Roman script with great accuracy and effect in its pronunciation as well as its literature; and the last I heard, it was agitating for a parliamentary measure to get Konkani declared one of the constitutionally recognized Indian languages.)

Our own version of Konkani operates more along the lines of Ogden Nash's mules which have no rules. Its erratic nasal diphthongs would defeat the most stalwart of phonemes. So it remains a hybrid anomaly, occasionally given to surprises. Though only a small percentage of the national population is literate, those who speak our kind of Konkani have come up with an amazingly consistent 100 percent literacy rate—a matter more of eccentricity than pride, really, since we have no written script of our own. Borrow one from another language, as the Goans have done, and what emerges on the page resembles nothing so much as a vast impediment of speech. (Yet this hasn't stopped occasional enterprising playwrights from producing witty soliloquys, radio plays, and even a full-length feature film.)

For me, possessing a mother tongue without a script affords a very specific personal space. When you are constantly preoccupied with putting things down on paper, it is a curious comfort to have recourse to one language where this is strictly impossible. Perhaps in consequence, I can never forget Konkani no matter how long I am away from its source. Sometimes nasal, sometimes full of a most fetching sweetness, it isn't the first language I learned, but it is the one that springs quickest to mind in moments of stress, or between sleep and waking, or to give instinctive voice to a need. "I'm hungry" or "I want to go home" are never so immediate in any other tongue.

There are other comforts intrinsic to the language itself. When you slide into it, you also slide into its habits of thought. It makes you . . . easy-going. No wonder, considering how even after centuries of localization it is still too casual and rootless to have evolved its own script. Speaking Konkani is an altogether slapdash and undemanding process. The vocabulary is rich in emotional and ritualistic connotations. It has some of the wry, palpable quality and humor of Yiddish, for example; a visceral knowledge, beneath, of being on the run. But if you embark on a discussion that involves words of more than two syllables, if it's an abstraction you want, you just reach out and help yourself to the absent phrase from the nearest language at hand. Never any problem.

Out among the newspapers on the front verandah, there is only one irascible old pedant who insists on speaking our Konkani in its purest possible form, without so much as a single suffix borrowed from any other language. After a couple of sentences he begins to sound like a comic turn; and in the end, the elders predict, he will die complaining no one ever took him seriously.

Apart from this exception, there isn't a trace of self-consciousness in the patterns of speech heard in these rooms, along the hallways, up and down the stairs. Even the inanities of baby talk come easy and unembarrassed in Konkani. But it has its quirks. Where other languages might tend to anthropomorphize, ours does the opposite. Every aspect of animal or vegetable life is scrutinized in minutely loving detail and then transposed to the human condition without a blink. "Whatever you do," one of the aunts cautions me in the kitchen when I spill the chili pickles, "do it s-l-o-w-l-y and carefully, like a cockroach inserting its whisker in a hole."

Listening to her, I realize how apt the term "mother tongue" is. This is a matrilineal heritage, making short shrift of the occasional pedant. Whenever clans gather, as they have now, for a wedding or a festival, there is sure to be one old lady in the house who has all the time in the world to listen and to tell. It is she and others like her who use our language with utmost panache, handing down a fine lunacy of proverbs and admonitions and similes you couldn't remotely begin to hear elsewhere. In no other idiom I know are gods and demons such intimate creatures, or ordinary phrases fraught with so much weight. "Slicing a vegetable" isn't just slicing a vegetable. It is an act that, performed by a pregnant woman during an eclipse, could deform the unborn child. Neither superstition nor overstatement, this: just space for the implicit and accepted connections made between the macrocosmic-microcosmic roundness of shapes: sun, moon, womb. Here is one more attribute of a wholly oral tradition in which the most casual remarks can take on the timbre and burden of inherited memory. No piece of knowledge is ever laid to rest. Sooner or later, some submerged experience or misfortune or wisdom or legend comes to the surface; and then even the occasion on which it is spelled out adds to its cumulative lore.

(For instance, a nearby linguistic group, speaking another version of Konkani *almost* like ours, calls us "Dung-feet," probably because some ancestor slipped on a cow patty.)

Tiruvannamalai

In this small southern town, clustered untidily at the foot of a holy hill, my brother and sister and I rediscover that idiom whenever we spend our school holidays with a favorite great-uncle and two great-aunts.

Their house is thatch-roofed, with a guava orchard next to it; nearby stands a famous hermitage where they go every day to hear lectures and discussions on the sacred texts. Then at night, after dinner, the two old ladies spread out mats on the front verandah and sit leaning against the wall to conduct postmortems on what they have learned. At such times the most impressive of Sanskrit quotations can't surpass the rolling dignity of our own dialect's *however*s and *nevertheless*es that usually flavor their disquisitions.

Lying there half-asleep with our heads on their laps, we hear those words flying back and forth above us—words we can chew like lozenges, or stretch, or spit, or repeat over and over in ceaseless discovery and delight, dizzy as a dog chasing its own tail. Even then, when our dialect has become palpable as the hill that piles darkly beyond the orchard, there is always the sound of some other language on the horizon.

Down the road comes a slow clop of hooves, and the creak of a bullock-cart wheel, with the never-understood words of the driver's song rising unsteadily up to the stars, as he sings at the top of his voice to keep the demons and the darkness away.

Delhi

After moving north, in our house we speak an average of four languages a day—Hindi to the local street vendors, Tamil to our South Indian cook, English to some friends, and an agglomerate of all three plus our own dialect to one another. As a mongrel habit, it is ineradicable: containing all the overtones, the evocative details that can suffuse a particular language in a particular setting, giving us a lore that may be finally not so different from that of the old women in the clan. Our lore is more anecdotal than legendary, that's all: spread thinner over more languages and paced perhaps to suit another generation, a changing and more mobile way of life. Like others whose backgrounds form a similar patchwork, we accumulate an inevitable fund of jokes we ourselves find hugely amusing even if no one else does—all based on the experiences of living with more than one language. On the most dreadful of interlingual puns and malapropisms; or long involved taradiddles about a misplaced householder who bargains with tradesmen using entire sentences uttered devastatingly in one language with the exact intonation of another; or haphazard, trilingual riddles and puzzles that descend to a frenzy of cheating all around.

In all of this, of course, how you originally meet up with a language has a lot to do with how you play its games afterwards. The rest of my family has what has rather disgustingly been called "linguistic virginity"—the knack of making minds blank, linguistically speaking, of retiring into the inarticulate and emerging once more in a new tongue. So they can manage to effect the smoothest of transitions wherever we go. My own encounters with languages are far less skillful. Invariably I stumble upon them at an eleventh hour of crisis to discover that an entrance requirement has just been changed, or a new school regulation set up . . . such rules finally ceasing just where my interest begins, so that, plodding on from there on my own, I acquire a bumbling devotion to the tongue, quite disproportionate to my original need.

Technically—here in the north—I am supposed to write Hindi and

English with equal ease. I can write Hindi alright; my trouble is I can't read it, except as a humiliatingly slow and laborious process. Doing essays for college means getting carried away, laying on all manner of allegories and conceits with a lavish hand—a pleasurable, headily irresponsible feeling, a total high. The hangover comes next day as I cower in the back row, biting my nails and getting sick to my stomach lest I be singled out to read what I have written. After a while, though, to use Hindi as an adult means of expression is to find that for me it is a gawky adolescent, all angles and elbows. Try to be mature, I sound bombastic; try to be simple, I sound puerile. At last, in what local educators call Advanced Hindi, peripherals drop away. When we tackle Shankara's Advaita philosophy, the language stands up gloriously to take its measure. By which time I am scholastically "done" with Hindi, leaving me conscious of a whole space of possibility that, given my limitations, one sorry lifetime is too small to fill.

The sounds and syllables of "pure" Hindi are as pure a joy. It is resonant with the medieval folk poetry of singing saints like Mira, Kabir, Surdas, Tulsidas, who had all the passion and pliancy to encompass a universe in a couplet. Spoken well and simply, here is a language still capable of a lovely lilting vehemence that can work for every contemporary idiocy, from the mush of film songs to the tub-thumping of politicians. But increasingly in the decades after independence there have been efforts to groom it into officialese. Among other things, it is injected with large doses of many-syllabled Sanskrit, as if to swell its national dignity—a wholly spurious and sesquipedalian process that fools nobody but its perpetrators.

An uncle of mine, who lives down the road, does take-offs on the orotund News in Hindi we hear on the radio. He can also perform other sleights of tongue. He puts a handkerchief into his linguistic hat and takes out a rabbit. He can juggle endlessly with languages, rotating four at a time in the air, while you sit open-mouthed, wondering how long he can keep it up. All our word games are nowhere near what he does. The frustration that goes with such delight, of course, is that I can illustrate none of this in English.

August 15, Independence Day. Everyone is flying paper kites in the orange-green-and-white of the flag. Everywhere you look, a million tricolors dance against the monsoon clouds. The air is filled with the sound of their tugging, papery slither.

Jamuns—small, acrid purple fruit—have ripened to a shine along each tree that lines our street. Children would pluck them if they had a chance, but the jamun-pickers have already arrived: a nomadic tribe, leasing whole avenues of trees at a time. They set up camp right there on the sidewalk. Babies sleep safely out of harm's way in hammocks slung out of old saris; women hold out an enormous sheet of once-white canvas; men climb up and shake the branches; and the jamuns rain down, staining the pale cloth purple with their juice.

After supper has been cooked on charcoal braziers and they've all gone to sleep, one man keeps watch—clacking at the trees with a long bamboo pole, and splitting the night with weird discordant yells to frighten away the fruit bats, with their ominous six-foot wingspan, that come swooping out at dusk to plunder the trees.

By dawn the pickers are back at work, speaking among themselves in a dialect that to me—perhaps because I am watching them at a remove— sounds every bit as glancing and acrid and purple as the fruit they have come to pick.

The human act in language.

Ellora

From lexical and linguistic space to space around voices. Here on the ancient sturdy Deccan plateau, Ellora—the eighth-century Hindu city of temples—has been hewn out of solid rock, over eight hundred feet high. Starting at the top of the hill, they carved their way down, the builders: hundreds of years . . . and hands . . . and lives. Only birds claim the silence now.

No human voices, presumable inheritors, can take that living place or assume its rights—merely scratch a few shallow interruptions, to be smoothed out soon enough by their departure.

Dimly, then, comes the acknowledgment of how a voice in the end must inhabit its space; how speech, at its most essential, is a treaty with silence.

Peterborough, New Hampshire

The wind blows down Concord Street. We can hear the ice floes melting on the Contoocook . . . *crackle-rush* . . . a sound both brittle and fluid as the river reshapes itself, curving around the end of our street.

Sarith and I stand talking on the sidewalk. She lives three houses up from mine, in a gaunt old Victorian split up into apartments, where a church group has found accommodations for her and four other refugees from Cambodia. We speak of her English class, taught by a mutual friend; Cambodian typewriters that allow three tiers to each letter of their alphabet; her job, putting computer chips together; her hopes of moving to Seattle if she can manage it. . . . And then it invariably happens. Whenever we, or other women from other countries, talk together—here in this lovely little New England town, or anywhere else in the country—we reach this point. The surfaces of the present crack open like the floes on the river and the past flows through, reshaping our speech, bringing our words to one more birth. Whatever renditions of English we might use, our lingua franca remains the language of our lives:

Two Women Talk: "Sokhom" Means "A Little Safety"

My sister name "Sokhom" mean
"A Little Safety." But she die.
They call me "Sol": good luck.
Then for twenty-four hour I die.

You?

Pol Pot match my neck and rib.

Match?

Fire. Neck and rib. See . . . here
and here. My parents take my
body to monk. Day . . .

. . . Night.

Twenty-four hour. Then he
call me "Sarith." Magic. Power.
He give my name to life. How
in India?

Sometimes if our first-born
goes or second or third, the
next we call "Murthoo":
Dead.

Ah, Cambodia also. Give bad bad
name so nobody look. That too.

That too.

Lines in the Dark

Pune

The fiction I am beginning to write here (*Afternoon of the House*) focuses, intensifies, my usual preoccupation with fusion and antithesis: space / substance, stasis / movement, silence / sound. I need to bring them down to their stringency, that uncompromising level of a human touchstone, without which they are merely so much verbiage.

This thing has to be written in the spaces between words, the spaces between incidents, so that even if I do deal with factual detail, even if I do delve into physical and mental landscapes, my concern is to try and speak without speaking. I want to get to the beginnings of definition. What is "holy"? What is "mad"? What is "healing"? What is "thief"? Eliminate all notions of *prowess* with words. Do away with that spurious, retrospective headiness of being articulate. Get down to the sources instead. Wrest them out of that silence / cry from which experience is born.

PUT INTO WORDS THAT MOMENT BEFORE YOU CAN PUT IT INTO WORDS. And of course that's an impossibility. How can I even presume to try? But there's the monkey on my back, saying: "How dare you not risk it?"

It's not just a question of technique: of demarcating that tightrope, perilous here, between *simplicité* and *simplesse*, between real simplicity and its sophisticated semblance. More. It's trying to keep that connection, in work as in life, between inner and outer—so that any epiphanies I may have the temerity to approach can truly become moments of extended privacy. . . . Extending into insight. And I hope into art. Even saying that here is spurious. In the writing, of course, I haven't that recourse, I have to *do* it. And how? is the question. Can I? is the question. And the monkey says: "So what's another pitfall? Stake your life."

Elephanta Caves

India for me is where these inner-outer connections remain strongest but are also most capable of being frayed, simultaneously reinforcing and undermining that private mantra, the line from the Hopkins sonnet: *what I do is me, for that I came.* There is no upholstery here. Against surrounding hunger or deprivation, you can't raise your voice in the most justified complaint, from a personal cry to a metaphysical protest, without feeling reduced to a kvetch. To have a roof over your head, a desk, a typewriter, is to go from guilt to fruitless apology. There is a point after which it's no use saying, "OK, we all have our sources, we all have our strictures." Won't wash.

Yet here, where bellies have to be filled first, art still has roots. In Elephanta, Ellora, Belur, Halebid, Mahabalipuram, Mount Abu, elsewhere, it isn't the obvious genius and grandeur and scope of the finished caves or temples that prove it as much as those abandoned and time-blurred carvings where your eye completes what the sculptor's hand began, what no one else perhaps can see quite as you do, so that the very seeing of it becomes an act of creative complicity between the past and the present, between the visible and the possible.

Pune

This fiction again, which I seem to unwrite as fast as I write. Struggling with its spaces even as I keep a wary eye on the external spaces that bring it to birth, to make sure even tangents won't ring false, won't be just tangents. Taking the manuscript from context to context—the watcher in the head never falling asleep. Yes. Insomnia. *Many must have it.*

How fortunate to be able to hole myself up here and work every day. A conch shell blows for somebody's morning prayer; children and neighbors come around, peering through the windows at this weird anomaly of a woman closeted with her typewriter, under a sky illimitably full of sun. Subservient to my monkey, I want to scratch and ask for peanuts.

Outside, the hills around town change all day, from blue to lavender to a deep drenched purple and then, after dark, to the exact tinge you see in the smudges of fatigue beneath a child's eyes. It is June; we are waiting for the monsoon to break. It has passed Sri Lanka. It has rounded the tip of our southern coast. Then the wind drops. How to describe it? Day following hot, breathless day; the inexorable parching, all color drained from the earth and the sky and the hills; the unspoken anxiety in everyone's eyes: "Please don't let the rains fail, please don't let the crops fail, please let our bellies be filled . . ."

The wind picks up, reaches Cochin on the west coast, gets as far as Bombay, and then stops again.

Early morning, my mother and I go up to the roof to watch a cloud above the mountains—small, purple-grey, no bigger than the proverbial man's hand. And there it stays. "You might as well get back to work," my mother says.

In my workroom, at some point I realize I have to turn on the light. Clouds have massed overhead. Suddenly, a breath of coolness courses through the trees . . . there's a roll of thunder (incredible timing) . . . and then *down* comes the rain. A roar rises from the whole neighborhood, as if from one throat. Street vendors put down their baskets, college students put down their books, everyone links arms and goes singing and dancing and clapping down the street. Children rush out into the yard or up onto the roof, whirling round and around like little dervishes, arms flung wide open, lifting their heads to drink the new rain as it falls.

Delhi

The Raos come to visit when they hear I am back in India. They have had two children since last we met, down south: a girl of seven, a boy of five, whose names—Kavita and Anand—translate to Poetry and Bliss.

Their parents have saved, to read to these children, a story of mine published when I was in college here, about what our concept of divinity seems to a child. Moved and amazed, I tell myself that we Indians, like heffalumps, have long memories. But the kids themselves remain reassuringly themselves.

Poetry says: "Did you write it all yourself?"

I say yes.

Then she says: "Do you collect feathers?"

I say no.

Bliss, meanwhile, leans out of our second-floor window and spits at strategic intervals to discourage any passing thief who might steal their car, parked below.

Roots beyond blurred carvings, by now, and not indigenous to us alone, by any means: this rootedness in living, which creates around it the ambulant space of a perspective where I take my oath again on what I have always felt: that I am not a Writer, capital W, only me writing, like me breathing or me puking.

And to say that is not to skim the agonized awareness of prices paid— the relentless and irretrievable cost. Odd, inevitable and perhaps repeated to extinction by now: how, when the sources of being human and being an artist are the same, their practice should have to be so compartmentalized. So damnably difficult bringing the two together; such (perhaps self-defeating) effrontery to demand the kind of totality that some of us do. Wanting fusion, you can become a battleground; trying to live completely, you can die in bits. But the necessity never stops. I have earned myself, strengths and vulnerabilities inextricably allied; it is only from there I can speak.

New York

In an unforgettable old record, Mahalia Jackson's voice tells you: *I can't sing one thing / and try to live another.*

Jim says: "How can I stand up and say another word, if I don't live what I believe?"

I think back, then, on the two-odd years I lived in this city, the "literary" names known and met. My own naive perfectionism perhaps, in wanting artists to be custodians of a cultural conscience, often aghast at the discrepancy between the quality of their character and the pretensions of their talent . . . a monstrous imbalance, palpable as a limp.

Now at the Chelsea, with plaster falling off the ceiling, Jim speaks of the difference between "having a value and pursuing it."

And by now too I know full well the ways in which art can arise out of a sense of deficiency—for without that mindful, tangible handhold on the human, we are perhaps amorphous creatures who take form when we make form.

Colorado

Our conversations in front of the fire, where one completes a sentence the other began:
"The inwardness of me—"
                    "—has to become the outwardness of art."

And speaking of how, when all your pores are open, so much bad can come in with the good:

"The easiest learners . . ."

　　　　　　". . . are the ones most harshly taught."
(Which is perhaps why nonessentials can also build around us?)

Referring to the kinds of poets who "don't leave tips," Jim says: writing is gratuitous when two words or sentences put together could penetrate life, and don't.

It is not so much the hacks you mind, then, as the intelligent ones who have deliberately vacated themselves to shine up a surface. Yet there are those of us for whom, for better or for worse, the basic problem of art is at what level you take life.

On the Boat from Santorini to Crete

Warm sweet wind. Standing on deck at nightfall—feeling utter and uncluttered—we watch the wake from the side of the boat: the way it swirls and spreads, thinning out into a fringe of foam . . . just one line of awareness against the encompassing dark.

(Until another wave, slantwise from the stern, intersects and disperses it.)

Delhi

Two months later. Scuttling around, running some errand, I realize for the first time in what seems like centuries that I am not bone-tired. Something is getting put back together. Perhaps a return to familiar slow deep rhythms: a kind of physical certitude: the look of the land and the ones I love—light falling over cheekbones and hills in the same language, defining its durability.

Not to deny lacunae, difficulties; but able now to weld them into a known perspective against which it is possible, briefly, to rest. Meanwhile the wary watcher-in-the-head watches out against lapsing back into any old states of domiciled intelligence.

I don't want to locate myself only by geography (however strongly I acknowledge its power and point), or books, or beliefs. I want to be located in every breath I take.

So . . . still . . . and any other guards and prepositions that come my way, being rested and rooted and strangely at peace now is like an extrapolation of that moment on the boat to Crete.

Here's a stillness too requisite, too voluntary, to be merely acquiescent. A living necessity, all too often denied to all too many of us: these moments of poise, balance, between taking in . . . and giving out.

To me this hiatus has always been a very specific though nameless dimension between what is fully received, and how you respond to it, what you *do* with it. Space for physical/mental/emotional impacts to make connection with what continues breathing inside us. Space that delineates too, I think, the difference between an abeyance and an abdication of intelligence:

Where you can afford to wait, open-eyed, open-pored, and *in* yourself totally—as clear as possible of any preoccupations that could blur a direct seeing. From where, having brought your whole unimpeded self to the moment, you can then carry your perception of it beyond the moment and beyond the self.

Started to spell it out—this region of absolute focus—and its place in my own life, for one, that night on the boat to Crete. But we docked and I couldn't follow it through. Now I think a real quest for metaphor (among so many other things) is tied up with it: nothing to do with verbal embellishments, not even merely expressing the abstract in terms of the concrete, but more: *a noting, a tracking down, of process into significance*. As with the line of foam on the sea to Crete that night, and its directing me (for one) to our edges of awareness in the dark.

Bainbridge Island

Several years later, on this other island in this other part of the world, I find myself following another line in the dark, this time tracking photography. So far—being a mechanical dimwit with a good eye—I have felt too intimidated. Now a blessed combination of people and events brings this dream to fruition: a dear friend gives me a camera for our shared birthday, my husband enrolls me in a six-week photography course, and marvelously witty Roslyn McWatters teaches it. Finding me in an otherwise dreary class, she claims she ran home crying: "There is a God, there is a God!" Toward the end of her course, more serendipity walks into the picture. Having developed some prints in Seattle, I'm looking over them while returning on one of the fat daily ferries that chug across Puget Sound when the woman next to me says: "May I see those?" I hand the prints across. After slow and careful scrutiny she hands them back, and asks: "Would you like a show?"

BOINNNNNG! . . . but humbling too—besides scary, when you remain fazed by all the technical aspects of the craft. Yet risking a solo exhibition, assembling the different ingredients of its theme ("Inscapes / Outscapes"), and—to my amazement—selling enough in this first show to get back what I put into it seem at times less salient than those inner / outer spaces involved here. The act of "seeing" for photography is of course like entering—no, not another element, but another facet of the same element. A different vocabulary, visual this time, responding to the same abiding and indefinable source of art. "Every tool carries with it the spirit by which it has been created," Heisenberg says in his *Physics and Philosophy*.

This "spirit" reveals a unity of expression deep enough to take in diversity—whether from one art to another or from one image to the next. Macro-photography gets you so close to daily sights and objects that they change their shape and yield a mystery. A paperweight can produce a phantom. Ten inches of sand on a lakeshore can become cloud and coast and water. Water itself, close up, will offer anything from quicksilver, to amoebas, to knots and knurls of wood, to molten lava. The patterns and transformations prove endless.

You learn the correspondence of forms in nature. Spots: from the shell of a calico crab to the pelt of a leopard. Spreading tendrils: from capillaries to tree roots to river deltas. Curvilinear shapes: from the sweep of a coastline to the billow of a cloud. From the sophisticated choreography of a dancer's mudra to the simplicity and suppleness of the human hand, to our shared and inherited curve of earth and space. . . .

Looking across at the Kitsap Peninsula from Bainbridge Island, I see glimmering ripples on the water that exactly echo fish scales. Microcosms and macrocosms hold hands; we confront fractals again. And all the varied impulses of the creative vision affirm an implicit affinity with the universe around us. Archetypes answer our vision no matter where we walk.

Capitola, California, and Peekskill, New York

Doing cover photographs for books of poetry by Jane Cooper, State Poet of New York, 1995–1997, uncovers more spaces: fusing landscape and language. Her revised edition of *Scaffolding* (1993) merits nothing less than the ocean floor off Capitola, where you can walk during the lowest tide of the year. Long tresses of seaweed lie strewn about undulant and glossy as the hair of the ghost in a Japanese tale told by Lafcadio Hearn. Underfoot, fossils of sea-creatures embedded in rocks glisten from a wave that might have washed over them five minutes or thirty-five million years ago. A flamboyant sunset, all flame and gold and scarlet, blazes across the ocean, gradually subsiding into a Monet palette of dun and rose, mauve and heliotrope, until that in turn dissipates into a sheen the color of light. Now as you look across the shimmer of wet sand you can't tell where the sand ends and the sea begins, or where the sea ends and the sky begins. It's like being inside a pearl. Dazed, I happen to glance down. There, spanning about twelve inches on the shores of the Pacific, held between tide and tide, is a perfect pattern of pale and dark sand, scaffolded together as rare and steadfast as Jane Cooper's work.

Her next book demands the idiom of snow. I walk the woods and hills of an old friend's family house behind Peekskill—clumping around in borrowed boots three sizes too large, while a hysterical poodle yaps at my ankles, scampering and peeing on any pristine patches of woodland we come across until it is finally shooed home. Then I am vouchsafed a gift:

Shadows beneath a single bare Japanese maple provide the exact force and visual approximation of *Green Notebook, Winter Road* (1994)—the intricate simplicity of the central image; those misty shadows in the snow, suggesting things not quite seen or heard; and then the long calligraphic line of a branch, like a road or a river seen from far, far above.

Davis, California

The unfolding years help to further an exploration of these regions that intersect the different arts. This time the solo exhibition I'm putting together, Image, Text & Context, consists of watercolors, collages, assemblages and text. The images are created with materials from different countries—birds' nest paper from Thailand, strands of alpaca wool and weaving from Peru, dried banana bark from the Philippines, handprints of seventeenth- and eighteenth-century paintings on wood from Gujarat, India, papyrus paper from Egypt, etc. The text accompanying the images summons up their various resonances of symbol and origin, and the context throughout is international. For I feel these collages are not just my doing: they are to honor the work of anyone under the Philippine sun who ever pounded a banana bark; or any of my fellow Indians who ever stamped a block print; or any child anywhere tracing a finger along a plant fiber that would one day become natural (not mass-produced) paper and reach someone on the other side of the world. It's all our history. We belong to it, and it to us.

Here, words and images can't merely illustrate but must *illuminate* one another to shape a joined wholeness of perception. Different forms of art come together from an interdisciplinary background. Designs echo the movements sketched in the air by the hand-mudras of classical Indian dance. Fragments of collage walk out of their frames and on to the accompanying text, to blend the visual with the verbal. And in wryly marking this fiftieth year of India's independence, these images also walk out of their own roots to affirm the kinship of art across all cultures.

Yet where is the precise space that starts a direction toward a new form of expression without abandoning the old? How far back does a seeming newness go, and what precipitates it? For me there are scatters and flashes from the past. Scraps collected across a peripatetic existence even when I didn't know their purpose, couldn't afford to be a packrat, and had to live light. Influences I hadn't known were influences. Et cetera. But the immediately impelling factor is an automobile accident.

On a quiet New Year's morning two years ago, a pick-up truck careens through a stop sign, rams into us from the side, fishtails, rams into us from the back, and smashes us headlong into a telephone pole, crumpling the car. I emerge smashed up enough myself to consider recovery a double blessing, for somehow at the end of a long and painfully arduous process I seem to have recovered more than I ever lost. When a critic covering the show asks me to describe my work in one word I find myself saying: "Prayer." Prayer not as asking but in affirmation: not only for myself but in an almost tactile kinship with everyone's ordeals everywhere—a joint and grateful celebration at having finally managed to come through.

Words and writing are ungainly here; only images will do. And they come showering down unbidden, one after the other, sometimes with scarcely time for each to be finished before the next begins. There's no conscious striving, only a kind of blessedly wordless harmony: a form of meditation leading to a pure place, a *pre*-place, where I am merely an instrument helping something *to become what it was meant to be*.

Nothing new. For of course this can also be true of any art, as of any deep endeavor: that still inner concentration akin to prayer. And it is writing after all that helps me to express this—enables me to speak as a practitioner from the inside out, not from the outside in, like those critics ("crickets," as Gulley Jimson calls them in *The Horse's Mouth*) or academics who—as artists know—are never at a loss for an empty word.

If I am delighted and amazed all over again at the show being a near sell-out (in fact I'm staggering around in a stupor of disbelief), that's food for the table, food for the stomach. What's food for the spirit is the response from most of those who come to see the show. For they answer the doubleness of any creative need / effort: expression through a self as well as communication to others. (Which can be such damnable agony when it is dammed up.) But here again now is that sense of human connection which began all this. As affirmed by the nine-year-old at the opening who, when her parents are leaving, wants to go around the gallery once more. "You've seen it already," her mother says. "But *Mom!*"—total outrage—"I have to *remember*." Or the old woman who stands very still before each canvas and finally asks: "Do you know why these are good?" Taken aback, I stammer: "I'm—I'm glad you think so. No, I don't know." She says slowly: "Because they're *needed*."

Referring to such assimilations and "internalizations" of art, Soetsu Yanagi in *The Unknown Craftsman* speaks of how when a work of art is truly apprehended, the viewer becomes the artist (sharing and participating in the act of creation—as with those time-blurred carvings on stone temples, where your eye completes what the sculptor's hand began). Yanagi's context is that of the Tea Ceremony, where a piece of pottery can lead you to draw out the hidden *shibui* beauty of utensil and ceremony from your own awareness, thus making an artist of the onlooker.

More, Yanagi takes this mergence even a step further. And to read him now, after experiencing the harmony of the *pre*-place, is like coming home. For he it is who can pinpoint that moment when "picture draws picture" and "cloth weaves cloth," when, past all pleasure or hazard, the duality between the worker and the work is totally dissolved.

Ann Arbor

This abiding influence has been incubating since college. A professor here mentions Soetsu Yanagi and his collection and concept of mingei— folk art that takes in the anonymity of the craftspeople, the daily usage of the craft, and above all the spirit that moves it: creating work not "made" but "born." We are told how the Japanese might test such pots, for instance. Not by delicate handling but by slapping them from hand to hand to see how well they stand it; by rubbing oily noses against them to see how well they absorb it; by filling them with mustard oil to see how well they store it. "The pot has to have humility, you see," the professor says. Over the years and against varying idioms—especially what T. S. Eliot calls "the cool beauty of ceramics," so many retaining their almost cathedral quality of stillness across the centuries—there remains the ghost of a mingei pot that can store mustard oil.

Shifts, Journeys, Transformations

On the Train from Mumbai to Pune

Crush and sweat and chaos of a second-class compartment. A blind beggar, with dholak-drum and cymbals, is singing the sixteenth-century songs of Tukaram as I've never heard them sung before. Chikki-sellers get on at Lonavla—chikki being the kind of ultimate peanut or cashew-nut brittle guaranteed to lock your jaws shut forever—and insist on thrusting the stuff under your nose. Shoeshine boys. The cha chap, complete with kettle of tea, cups and a washing bucket. Cleaning methods are of the utmost abbreviation: each used cup is dipped in the same water, swished around with a forefinger, and then refilled for the next customer.

Opposite me, a boy of about six travels with his father. The father is grey-haired but young-faced. His luggage consists of a single cloth bag filled with all the paraphernalia for preparing betel leaves, including nutcrackers for the supari: do-it-yourself with a deafening vengeance, for he keeps exploding the betel nuts at intervals throughout the journey.

He scarcely speaks to his son, but watches over him gently and unobtrusively all the time. Hauls him to the upper berth to sleep the moment his eyelids start to droop; gives him chikki or crisp, savory chivda without waiting to be asked, as if gauging exactly how long it will take the child to get peckish—anticipating his needs, and neither starving nor glutting them. When father speaks to son at all, it is to admonish him in low tones: Take off your sandals if you want to put your feet up. Don't step on the lady's typewriter.

Yet whenever the boy is intrigued or struck by anything—from beggar to tea-vendor to chikkiwalla to an airplane outside or the sudden engulfing dark of the tunnelways through the mountains—he turns and makes round eyes at his father, and the father half-smiles back as if the whole changing context was a conspiracy hatched entirely between the two of them.

I find myself extraordinarily moved by that. Especially after having spent the past year in a culture that is so *vocal*, to see the essential voicelessness of their bond, the speech of their silence, their Sumi space in the jam-packed compartment.

On the Delhi-Mumbai Rajdhani Express

The train slows down, going past Bharatpur and the bird sanctuary. September. Even at a distance, and even just travelling through, why do we feel so shamelessly rooted to this stubborn, intransigent soil of ours?

("If it isn't drought over there, it's cyclones," a Westerner once remarks dismissively to me, and I want to hit him.)

The floods have receded, leaving stretches of water standing about, reflecting a million sunsets underfoot—one for every pool and puddle and ditch—until you can scarcely tell earth from sky.

And here are the birds now. Adjutant cranes; egrets; immense herons; kites; solitary swallow-tailed drongos; a cloud of weaver birds, with their nests hanging like wicker-covered, upside-down Chianti bottles from every branch.

The train stammers along, impeded by signals, and then comes to a stop. The sunset dims to just an amber sheen lying over the land, but everything is *told* in that light: every leaf and hollow and twig. . . . Still dimmer. Silhouettes take over. Tall kans grass, blades etched precisely black as in a Japanese print, but ending in high tossing plumes of white that hold the afterlight and sway luminous as torches (they're shaped like that too) long after all is dark around them. At that moment, a flock of wild white doves flies above—so absurdly, identically lucent that even their silhouettes are white!

This is what our landscape keeps doing to some of us. Takes our vision and turns it inside out: conferring, contradicting, leaving us never the same again. Yet there are others who think it is monotonous, which it can be; and cruel, which it is.

First Trip on an American Railroad

I have exactly sixteen dollars in my pocket and exactly two people I know on this continent, neither living anywhere near my destination— the University of Michigan at Ann Arbor, to which I have won an international scholarship that is high on prestige and low on funds. Having landed in New York, I now take this train.

It skirts the Hudson River all the way north to the station where I shall get off, en route, to attend an "orientation" program at Bard College, though clearly what I need most at this point is to be occidented a bit.

Meanwhile I don't want to miss any detail of this exotic journey, and get astigmatic trying to squint between the mapped patches of dirt on my window pane. A cartographer's delight, this smudgy window pane. And the trains here smell different. No dust, just plain stuffy fug. But the river—oh, the river.

Odd, how foreigners are always being bombarded with the superlatives of a country. In the USA, for instance. Skyscrapers: WHEW! The Grand Canyon: WOW! What eludes advertisement, thank goodness, is the everyday bread-and-butter beauty of the land. These low hills on the opposite bank, dipping their shadows into the water; bridges filigreed by distance until their massive girders loom overhead; the way gestures and intonations and meetings and partings fall into this setting. . . .

After a while I am like a saturated sponge, I can't take in another drop. When I sit down to be occidented at dinner and am faced with a carton of milk, I wonder what the hell you're supposed to do with it. All it says is: "Open." But where? How? Given all the angles converging on the explanatory arrow, from which direction do you tackle it? I scrutinize the thing from top to bottom, bottom to top, upside down and diagonally. It remains "a little study in infinity, with no beginning and no end."

At last I ask my neighbor on the left. He shows me. He is from East Africa, I think, and has been in this country for two weeks, and knows the ropes.

It's drizzling in Ann Arbor once the train gets there. I find my way to the campus and sit on one of the benches at the Diag, warming my gloveless fingers, to wait for my contact from the International Center. Instead, a stranger appears, says: "Nobody, not even the rain, has such small hands," and disappears. I never see him again. Not once during the rest of my college years in this town.

Gora, Japan

When serious illness interrupts my degree at Ann Arbor, I join my father, who also happens to be returning to India via Japan after heading a delegation abroad. One weekend we stay in this little town, tucked away beyond the folds of the mountains that hide it from touristy Hakone.

The house—"traditional Japanese"—is not actually in town, nor even on its outskirts. It stands by itself, complete and quiet; which is how it makes you feel as you enter.

The place has been partitioned unpretentiously off into two sections—one large, one small—in a way that reduces the whole notion of "rooms" to absurdity. The interior space is sometimes defined, as at home in India (where exactly you leave your footwear by the front door, where you turn to find the alcove with its scroll and flowers); but for the most part it remains itself, retains a serenity that comes from accommodating the structures of living without having to change the spareness of its own shape. Where you eat by day—on the low table brought in for meals and then taken away—is also where the beds are

57

spread out to sleep at night, with a flexibility that fits like flesh around the bone.

I know my surface tenure as a guest but am guiltlessly grateful for it, since that is the space I have been apportioned. As I am grateful for my friend, the landlord's daughter, who doesn't know a word of any language I do, and vice versa; yet we can talk for hours with hands and eyes, and she gets me into kimonos and I get her into saris, and we find it the hugest joke in the world.

Nowhere else have I felt this blithe and unapologetic removal from the known. Despite my recent brush with mortality, when watching the road that curves its way up through the hills, I can fool myself into believing fate can't touch me here.

That night, sleeping by the enormous porcelain urn that holds coals glowing to keep us warm, I hear the beginnings of a rumble. Instantly I know what it is. Earthquake! And whether or not this beautiful house can withstand it, as it has over the years, I am a jelly of fear—but can't merely lie there and don't want to waken my father unless it is serious. All the while the rumbling gets louder, nearer. So I disinvolve myself from my bedclothes and slide the door fractionally open to see what is happening outside.

Nothing. A truck is climbing up the curving road and my earthquake is put in its place.

South India

Clearly such shifts between the expected and the actual, between certain perceptions and apperceptions, are old familiars which have been going on for a long time.

As children we've tried training our eyes to see what in our dialect is called Black Sunlight, which hints at the coming of rain. What is this subtlety so visible to the elders and not to us? Day after day we keep pestering them: *Is the sunlight black today?* And sometimes it is, and sometimes it isn't, while we peer up at a dazzle that, to us, seems as unremitting as ever.

Then one day I see it: A curious edge to the shadows; a dense dark between leaf and leaf, or under trees. The glare that blurs all outlines has gone, leaving the light as dense as the dark.

Tiruchirapalli

Memories of going to the temple as a child. The physicality of the experience, which stays with me still. A gigantic gopuram gate, carved every inch, with scenes from mythology—many too high to be deciphered from below. At the threshold, a huge golden step I have to hop across, right foot first. Inside, the passageways that have to be traversed left to right, all the way around. (Circumambulating—so that you not only honor the central shrine but *contain* it. . . .) The significance of the sanctum sanctorum being called *garbha-griha: Garbha* meaning womb, *griha* meaning home. Not just the womb but the home of the womb: the source.

Near the entrance stands a pillar with a frieze of elephants around it, at just about my height; trunk curling into tail curling into trunk. . . . I keep running my hand along them, around and around the pillar, until they are part of my palm and my palm is a part of them. A private ritual. Each time. Wordless. Having to know what it is like to be an animal before you can enter a shrine.

There, the smoky erratic flicker of oil lamps probes but never dispels the dark. When the priest starts to chant, his voice rises and echoes and melts away, into the shadow, into the stone. And when he stops, the silence is as sculptured as the stone.

It is as if all boundaries have disappeared: between solid and void, light and dark, sound and stillness; between you and what you see. Gone. Beyond logic or possibility.

Davis, California

A barely comprehended Sanskrit verse returns with another resonance after I've undergone some serious and massive surgery. Considering the phantom pain and twitch of amputated limbs, and confronted by the missing bits in my own inner anatomy, I find myself welcoming back their essential presence, appreciating their having sacrificed themselves so the rest of me can survive. Metaphorically it revivifies that Sanskrit verse about wholeness, which begins: *purna mada, purna midam.* . . . It makes me see that somehow one must regain wholeness in order to retain wholeness. Doesn't come easy, but it also brings a reminder that our body after all is our oldest friend, sticking by us since birth. The luckier among us may dismiss it or mortify it or overgratify it or grumble at it (too fat, too thin, etc., especially in a culture where health becomes a morality and commerce panders to its obsessions), entirely forgetting the wholeness of that old and sensible companionship.

The Mysore-Ooty Road

Why should certain seemingly uneventful journeys from the past continue vividly unchanged into the present, as if set in unalterable aspic? More than twenty years ago I take a solitary and rattling hundred-odd mile bus ride from the city of Mysore to the hill station of Ootacamund (Ooty) in the Nilgiri or Blue Mountain ranges of South India. The significance of the trip, if any, perhaps lies only in its having been yet another witness to lives that touch and do not touch in transit. Some trips have a way of thumbing their noses at significance—even any personal significance that might wait at journey's end to mark the destination.

To those of us who spent parts of our childhood in the Nilgiris, as Vrinda Kumble and I agree, these Blue Mountains have an omnipresent, almost prototypical quality. Suddenly—when she is at a conference in Australia or I am climbing a hill in California—cold air can smite our skin with a remembered tang: something compounded equally of damp earth, woodsmoke and eucalyptus. And our immediate surroundings at once invoke an implicit one, and we find ourselves exclaiming "Just like the Nilgiris!" No need of any Scotty to beam us aboard; we're there already.

Hitherto, for both our families, the usual and longer approach from Madras and the east coast has also been the more dramatic: dizzy with contiguous hairpin curves swiveling up the Western Ghats as they tower straight up, eight thousand feet, from the plains to the sky, dwarfing the tiny railway station of Mettupalayam with its toy train that chuffs picturesquely up the slopes, past even tinier stations with names like Arranmore and Lovedale and Wellington. (For at the top, at that altitude, about ten degrees north of the Equator, lies the climate of a mild English summer: immured in another kind of nostalgia, this time for members of the post-colonial Raj. As children, we've heard those who Stayed Behind enumerate the glories of the three hill-stations in the area: "In Kotagiri you live to be eighty; in Coonoor you live to be ninety; in Ooty you have to be shot.")

The Mysore-Ooty Road bears no such sediment or overlay for me, whether of longevity or otherwise. I've never been on it before. This approach is less steep, beginning as it does in South India's central plateau and heading for the rim of the Bandipur jungles. Soon forest gives way to plantations of teak in flower: fistfuls of cobwebby dirty-white blossom against their background of deep, gigantic leaves. Then rice in the valleys, growing tender and jewelled here, unlike its intense green in the plains. Scarlet trumpets of hibiscus everywhere. Octroi barriers where trucks and buses come to a lumbering stop in front of a rickety bamboo pole laid hopefully across the road—as if a child's elbow couldn't have knocked it off—while authorities from the checkpost run out to confer with the driver. Sleepy-looking authorities they are too, whom you catch in tableaux as you pass, rewinding their turbans, picking their noses or waking up from a nap, making grumbly faces over their ledgers before waving you on again.

I wonder who else lives around these checkposts, since one sleepy authority can't account for a whole village. All those trim little houses with bamboo gates in front and their gardens crammed with cannas and marigolds; where plantain clumps shake their tattered leaves over the kitchen wall, and vines are trained to grow along the roof until they burst into fat yellow pumpkins on the staid grey thatch.

Turn a corner and that checkpost village is completely gone, pumpkins and all. You're in a bamboo forest now, swimming through aqueous light from the feathery upcurving sprays of green and gold overhead, while the roadside below is punctuated by red anthills growing higher than a person—whole termite cities, their spires and towers steepled together like praying hands.

A few more corners, a mammoth grinding of gears, and the bus has reached Gudalur, with its bust of Mahatma Gandhi—painted aluminum—in the middle of the market square. (Does that bust still exist? Or has it been knocked down in a riot, or given way to immortalize one corrupt pot-bellied politician or another?) Meanwhile the Mahatma presides over a regular rest stop, where travellers buy tiny hill bananas or tea or snacks, and refuel, and check brakes, before anything on wheels can attempt the ghat section ahead. From here you are supposed to get your first close-up glimpse of the Nilgiri mountains. What you actually see are clouds, clouds, and more clouds, lowering their fat white bottoms to obliterate entire villages and tea slopes at a time.

For tea has taken over after bamboo left off. Acres of rounded shrubs, highlighted here and there by the smoky glint of silver oaks planted in rows for shade. And then wildflowers. Brilliant blue four-o'-clocks and convolvulus. Sunflowers flung carelessly across the edge of a precipice, cutting yellow patterns in the sky. Poinsettias pricking out the hillside like bright drops of blood. Cinchona trees sometimes flashing leaves dabbed in sunlight with that same red, often as not sheltering the roof of a quinine factory next door.

Each of the small towns along the Ghat Road has such a raison d'être of its own—quinine (against malaria), or tea, or a hydro-electric project, or even the manufacture of needles—though there's no immediately distinct result to show for it. Most of the towns look alike. Roofs of wood . . . or tile . . . or corrugated iron sheets held down by bricks . . .

are stacked pell mell as if one on top of the other, to follow the line of the road, which in turn crookedly follows the line of the land, and explodes on occasion into Sunday markets clamorous with turbans and saris and squalling infants.

Relentlessly, you know you are just passing through. Once, when the driver stops for a cup of tea in one town, I see a frieze of faces through the tea-shop window. Grubby panes, steam rising from the metal tumblers, and those faces emerging in half-curtained fragments to reveal a moustache here, a chin there, a sudden gesture from a gnarled and work-hardened hand.

Outside women bargain, vendors shout their wares, and a magnificent oblivious madman with matted hair and the bearing of an emperor walks his way in and out of the crowds, declaiming to the mountains.

Santorini, Greece

Sitting on the parapet edging the roadside outside a taverna, waiting for it to open. Seen from this high hillside, looking down: a solitary street lamp, blinking on and off; Greek rooftops, flat and white and passionately geometric, angled steep against hurtling cliffs; and the Burnt Islands in the caldera just a smudge on the water, when earlier they had been silhouetted black—like piles of wet charcoal—on an incandescent sea. To my left a pliant eucalyptus sapling whose leaves swim like minnows in the wind. . . . The whole tree moves and bends and makes self-deprecating gestures, then throws itself back with the abandonment of total laughter.

Wonder, then, whether—as in my mother tongue, Konkani—the whole notion of anthropomorphism isn't taken back to front. Whether we humans aren't the ones who follow the shapes and lines of natural objects when we most spontaneously express an emotion. Whether—as clearly it so often does—the dynamism of dance comes from precisely this kind of congruence.

What happens when such congruence is given no accommodation? Is stunted and strait-jacketed by implicit and explicit demands of one sort or another? Culture. Decorum. Tyranny.

Venice

In San Marco Square:	After her bad marriage, Bianca refuses any more to be essentially adjacent, like the Logetta at the side of the Campanile.
In the park by Ca'D'Oro:	Hat on an empty bench, man's hand on girl's thigh as he talks of something else: absentee landlordship.

Suddenly mirrored acquisitions and appropriations of space.

Upstate New York

Back in this country again, the view from the tower window stretches across formal lawns and fountains to the valley beyond, rimmed on the horizon by the Green Mountains of Vermont. At the nearer end of the lawn there is an enormous, battered old maple whose top branches, bare and lyre-shaped, invite transformation.

Birds . . . mourning doves, swallows, blunt stubby little starlings, once a scarlet tanager, once a speckled hawk, once a cardinal . . . come to perch there, arranging themselves with such casually immaculate asymmetry that the sky behind them turns to silk, every twig is brush-stroke dark, and they have designed a Sumi scroll by their very presence.

Downstairs in this big old house where we all work separately and together, Sally shares the becoming of her book, leaving each new poem at the top of the steps for each new day we look and learn and walk and talk together. So deeply, with her: "The gift of poetry is the innocence to sing."

Bainbridge Island

Even being still on an island can be a movement. Light says different things on an estuary, and the water answers as the land cannot. Wind and tides keep adding to that vocabulary, of course, and when you take ferries from island to peninsula to island again you participate in a larger movement of change, constant and intrinsic to the landscape.

Whidbey Island, northeast of us, affirms that change. There the trees don't come up so close and steep to the edge of the road and the edge of your eyelashes. And "vistas" don't wait to open up until you've reached the water's edge. On this much larger island you can come upon an expanse of farmland or pasture that shelves gently away to a hidden horizon; and the shoreline accommodates areas very much like the salt marshes of the East Coast. During our late summer visit all the grasses have mellowed to the exact tint and texture of ripe wheat. Wildflowers tumble down hillsides right into backyards and street corners until the whole landscape seems stitched together by these delicate filaments of color.

Our destination, an old farmhouse on the southern coast, boasts a stunning location. It overlooks a gradual slope of meadows stretching down to salt marshes that edge what is endearingly known as Useless Bay. Across the bay we can see the drama of a storm building up layer on layer, all purple and dazzling silver, turning Seattle's distant downtown into a fantasy of toothpicks beneath it.

On our return trip, the ferry ride westward to Port Townsend carries the same magic. At first the water is truly like silk: so sensual, so smooth, every liquid dark curve flowing into the next. Then suddenly, about halfway through the journey, it puckers. Maybe from the winds blowing through the straits? Maybe from the tides? The surface has become cross-hatched with lines as fine and dignified as wrinkles on a parchment skin—almost sacerdotal, as beautiful as the previous smoothness, and somehow merging harmoniously into it. Against this, when we swing into harbor, all the old Victorian houses of Port Townsend suddenly turn into a stage set, setting off a dazzle of reflections in ocher and red and wood and brick and gold.

Transformations here continue beyond landscapes and seascapes. Shape-shifters take form in the art and legends of the Arctic and sub-Arctic peoples on both sides of the Bering Strait and down the Pacific Rim. A seventh-century wood carving from Kodiak Island shows a man becoming a bird. Behind glass at an exhibit, it depicts a bas-relief consisting of two fluid triangles set one on top of the other. The human face lies below, all its lines pulled craggily downward by gravity. Above an invisible jointure, the bird face in profile soars into powerful flying lines that make you *feel* the beat of wings without having to see them.

Just northward up the west shore where we live, the channel between Bainbrige Island and the Kitsap Peninsula is called Agate Pass. Masked dancers and storytellers among the Native Americans of the Pacific Northwest tell the story of a young girl who lived on the banks of Agate Pass.

Her name (as I hear it) was Yokanta, and she was so beautiful that young men came from miles around to court her. But she would have nothing to do with them. She preferred clamming on the banks, spending hours happily by herself. One day a young man came out of the sea and walked right past her. Yokanta was not used to being ignored. She was intrigued at first, and then attracted. Picking up her basket, she went to take a closer look at the man. He was unlike anyone she had ever known, luring her as no one ever had. They talked together while he helped her with her clams; and as her basket slowly filled, she came to know he loved her as she loved him. But she could be his wife only if she fulfilled two conditions. One: she would have to leave with him at once, without going home to say goodbye to her family. Two: she could return to visit them only three times, no more.

Yokanta finally agreed. Hand in hand they walked out into the sea. The water rose higher and higher, from their waists to their throats to their eyes to a level that rose farther and farther above their heads. She found she could breathe quite easily, and she began to live with him in his land under the ocean.

At this point the masked dancer takes over the story of her three return visits to her village on the banks of Agate Pass. Yokanta emerges with her back to the audience, crouched low and cloaked by a blanket of traditional design in brilliant red and black and pearl-white. As she turns, her cloaked hands are crossed high above to hide her face. When she slowly parts them it becomes visible bit by bit: the mask of a stylized sea bird with an elongated beak. The same dance is repeated for the second visit: this time her face has become that of a water-creature like an otter. And the third time it is HUGE, transformed into a sort of sea lion, towering over her slight body.

As she vanishes behind a black curtain, the storyteller comes out to resume his narrative:

The first time Yokanta returned her people were puzzled, not recognizing her. The second time they were wary. The third time they were frightened. Children ran away.

But Yokanta remembers she was once human, and will not let them go hungry. Now when she comes to Agate Pass she is invisible, but she guides the salmon to their spawning grounds, and gentles the clam-spirits so that they may provide food for the people she still loves.

When I tell my brother this story, I find myself starting to weep. Yes, Yokanta also gentles those among us who, for one reason or another, have had to reassemble our molecules and undergo a drastic sea-change in our lives. She gives us the succour and sustenance of kinship—recognizing the heartbreak of becoming unrecognizable to those we cherish; understanding what it means to be uprooted past norms of gender or culture or belonging; knowing the prices to be paid for being in thrall to choices and circumstances, let alone cataclysms; yet celebrating a love that somehow stubbornly lasts into survival.

San Francisco

Observing all the blazoned transitions from an old year to a new can be the most boringly predictable exercise in alternatives. Either you're asleep or awake, marking time or ignoring it, squirming at resolutions or being stalwart about them, raising a glass on one continent, dismissing it on another, and so on. This time instead of spending the occasion quietly at home we happen to spend it quietly at a hotel, a couple of blocks from Union Square. (One nervous guest there is to describe next day how she and her children approach the square near midnight but find so many champagne corks popping and so many sidewalks wet with spilled beer that they beat a prudent retreat back to the hotel.)

This year I especially want to greet not only those I care about (who in any case remain curled snugly around my third rib, New Year or no) but also those whom I don't know at all. Standing at the window and hearing the sounds of the city, I become aware of all the people outside: some dressed up and festive, others trying desperately to survive in the streets, like so many stretched around the world . . . in India, Africa, Bosnia, Brazil, everywhere. A friend has left a candle on the table, and I light it in a prayer beyond words. Yes: Peace—Shalom—Shanti—all that and so much more.

Then, as if materializing right out of my thoughts about greeting those I don't know, a marvelous thing happens. From our window I can look across a low intervening rooftop into the many lighted windows of an apartment house opposite. So I wave at all the unknown people in there, to wish them well in my heart. And three kids silhouetted in a bright window on the eleventh floor wave right back. To make sure, I wave with both hands. They wave back with both hands. I make a huge circle with my right hand. They make a huge circle with theirs. I jump up and down. They jump up and down. Three laughing stick-like little figures in skinny jeans and tops, probably about eight and ten and twelve or thereabouts. Suddenly clichés boomerang back into truth. *There* they are, growing up into the coming year and years, heaven willing, long after we're dead and gone; and *there's* a gibbous moon tilting up and off to the left in the sky; and *there* it is, that sense of an abiding connection with the curve of the earth, and a well-wishing for all the lives upon it.

Singing Saints and Others

Pune

One of our most famous vocalists frequents this neighborhood; another lives in it. At this time Hirabai Barodekar must be sixty-odd, looks forty-odd, though chronology is irrelevant. She may have passed the professional peak of her career, but seems to have reached some other acme, equally important. It isn't only a question of performances. Walking into that house is like walking into music.

Her accompanist needs special care. He is so mentally impaired, the story goes, that if he is led in to take his bath he just stands and looks at the water.

She adopted him when his parents died, maybe because she spotted what no one else had. He can't read a note, can't recognize a raga; but put any musical instrument in his hands and he knows beyond knowledge, plays like an angel, mopping and mowing.

Delhi

My twin friends are both engaged to foreigners—one of whom lives in the farthest regions of the Eastern hemisphere, the other in the farthest West. They say they reach through in their minds to their dear companions whenever the city sleeps here and the night is still, past the obstructive muddle of days and distance. Then geographical space is not an enemy that separates but an element that links them to their lovers in a way that roads and bridges cannot, simply because those are so definitive and contained.

One night, standing at the window in the dark, the twins are conscious only of this separate link and a stray passerby or two: the angle of the street-lamp making exaggerated stilts of their shadows. Then a miracle occurs. A pair of Pahari (hill) acrobats goes by, one playing the flute and the other dancing to its tune. All by themselves, there in the middle of the road in the middle of the night.

The flautist merely walks along, playing, but his companion turns somersaults and cartwheels. And so does his shadow . . . and so does the tune. . . . It skims along and turns turtle and pokes into corners and rushes back and lifts itself up and skirls away. . . . And they slide into mush and think: yes, this is for the likes of us, for all acrobats and lovers who are alone and apart at night, anywhere on the face of this earth.

London

The first symphony I have ever heard, live. Going from Covent Garden out into the obedient greys and greens of an English countryside, marvelling at the whole notion of a *rest* between movements. At that space which can exist as an entity in itself.

Especially since there is no such thing in our classical music. If a vocalist were to miss a beat, he would sing the next in double-time or catch up on the third, to fit the exigencies of the tala or rhythm cycle. Only when he has finished singing does his voice overflow its sound; and the aftermath has a caught silence, richer for what existed before.

It is as if in Western music, silence can be poured into sound; in ours, sound is poured into silence.

New York

Manitas de Plata—the gypsy flamenco guitarist whose name translates to "Little Hands of Silver"—has finally agreed to perform abroad; here in the city, at Carnegie Hall.

We are about the earliest to arrive, and my companion has plenty of time to get antsy: as much in anticipation as in exasperation, grumbling away at the formality, the grandiose scale of the setting for an art so spontaneous, so intimate, such a passionate birthplace of *duende*.

But Manitas de Plata appears, and starts to play . . . and plays . . . and plays. . . . And a Spanish contingent on the balcony throws roses; and Salvador Dali, who is in the audience, stands up and waves his cane;

and by the end of the concert, Carnegie Hall has shrunk until it is no bigger than those little hands of silver.

Mumbai

After a particularly difficult month, I remark to my sister: "So eat, drink and be manic, tomorrow we depress."

She, with her infallible instinct for remedy, reminds me that Bhimsen Joshi is giving a concert this evening.

This is the other singer of the Pune neighborhood. Our best vocalist and now, at this period in his life, a magnificent lush. So it's bound to be chancy. If he has too much, he is hours late and cannot sing at all. Too little, then the spark is missing; a pedestrian exercise. Just right, then, just right. Untold. Unimaginable. Nobody like him.

As my sister and I set off for the concert, a priggish relative says: "He drinks too much."

I say: "Maybe the burden of his genius is sometimes too great for him to bear."

She says: "You think too much."

The concert is held in the open, next to the J. J. School of Art, and arranged as a Bharatiya Baitthak, "Indian seating": in effect, sit-as-we-sit-in-India (Bharat). Cotton durries have been spread on the ground and laid with long, glimmering white rows of mattresses and bolsters. Off at one corner there is a splendid old mango tree, but splendid old mango trees can be infested with red ants whose bites are vicious. We are carrying a fat thermos of coffee between us lest the music should go on until dawn. I yank at this elegant burden and suggest "Ambo?" meaning mango. My sister yanks back and rhymes "Yambo!" meaning red ant. Enticed, nevertheless, we make our way over and settle down.

There are no red ants. There is slug, leaving its slimy trail along the roots. Today's wait is half, maybe three-quarters of an hour long. When Bhimsen Joshi arrives he asks first for a few minutes of silence, in memory of two famous singers who died this month: one of "old age," as they say, and the other in a gratuitous and senseless accident. We rise and stand . . . still . . . together; heaven knows how many of us. The silence gathers.

Soil. Privilege to be part of the soil from which this music now grows. He begins with Darbari Kanada, a raga which to me is always mourning incarnate, no matter how the miniatures paint it or what the experts say. He begins to elaborate, to improvise, around every note, starting at the lowest possible register—which, given his range, is . . . "Tasmania?" my sister whispers, pointing down. After that we have no more words. Slowly, spellbindingly slow and intricate, the improvisations of the notes of the aalaap mount the scale, until our waiting for him to touch the top of the octave becomes a cliffhanger. When he finally does reach it, I finally draw breath and open my eyes, and see, through the branches of the mango tree, my first star. Sound made visible.

Too much! And there is more. The moment when I realize, hazily, that everything is a part of this listening . . . even the traffic on the main road behind us, even the scabrous old buildings all around . . . and a leaf dislodges itself from the mango tree and floats down to land in front of the microphone. The moment when I turn to exchange glances with my sister, and take in, beyond that beloved exquisite face, rows upon rows upon rows of others with exactly the same expression which, I now realize, has been making my own rapt face-muscles ache for the last four hours.

He makes faces too, singing. And his hands gesticulate, expressing the notes—hard to tell a singer from a dancer, sometimes, in this trance. The aalaap is over, the slow development of the vilambit, the quatrains of the khayal . . . now his improvisation launches into the sheer musical acrobatics of the taans—hurtling, dizzying arabesques that his hands weave into blurs. At the end of one sequence he brings those hands to rest, opening, giving, to the tanpura-player on his right. (Here. You take it.) Then another sequence, even more dazzling, and he offers it to the tabla-ji on his left. (For you.) And finally, with both hands, the most magnificent of all, to the audience . . . take, take. . . .

Over the applause that will not stop and will not stop and will not stop, those same hands continue upward, to rise and pause in the age-old gesture of the singing saints and street minstrelsy: palms closing around invisible castanets. Those singing saints after all have cut a swathe through centuries (from the eighth to the nineteenth), and professions (from Kabir the weaver to Surdas the potter to Mira the queen). Now Bhimsen Joshi embarks on the song I hadn't even dared hope he would sing: *Teertha Vitthala.*

Again the inevitable rightness of it, that classical concerts should end with the simplicity of these old devotional songs everybody knows— when the music has broken down all the sealed limits between people, and a medieval tune can take on the intimacy of a conversation between friends. *Teertha Vitthala, kshetra Vitthala* . . . the crowd has become a giant child, his voice the hand that strokes it.

When he finishes, we stumble up, dazed, speechless (ungainly thermos still between us), humming *Teertha Vitthala.* At the gate, the ticket-seller is stacking receipts into rhythmic piles, in time to *Teertha Vitthala* burbled under his breath. In the parking lot, students are revving up their motor bikes, sliding their feet on the pavement to every second beat of the melody. As we inch our way out, the morning street sweeper twirls his broom like a moustache, accenting every end-line, beginning-line, end-tune, end-night, always-night, always-day of the song, and yes, everything is a part of it.

Chennai

In our childhood a South Indian teaching North Indian music is a rarity. Mr. Murthy, as I'll call him, is a rarity in other ways as well. People whisper about him, we never quite know why, but the whispers include respect. Very strict. High standards. No nonsense. Though once there had been some nonsense. Whisper whisper.

When he arrives to confer with the grown-ups about singing lessons for a few of us in the neighborhood, we are tactfully banished upstairs and of course hang out of the windows trying to get a glimpse of the man. First off, he is so handsome it's dizzying. Second, third, fourth, fifth, and always, he is tiresomely dedicated. If we sing well he nods that handsome head up and down; if we make mistakes he shakes it side to side. No more, no less. In his music room the only requisites are a tabla, a tanpura, and a tenacity unswerving enough to match his own. He can spend an entire lesson honing the same note, then get up at hour's end and walk off without a word.

The whispers in time become conversations and inevitably we eavesdrop, for all the difference it makes to our stringent lessons.

"It's as if he is encased in armor."

"He has to be, after all—"

"Yes, but pity the man, he is human." From the tone we gauge the possibility of pretty girls, but that fizzles out.

"Considering his excellence, the concerts, the radio, why should he even bother to teach?"

"Well listen, how many openings can there be for a northern singer in the south? Even a genius has to earn a living."

"At least if he could find a single good pupil to pass on the tradition of his gharana. . . ."

"How do you know he doesn't have a single good disciple?"

"Maybe, but imagine someone of his caliber teaching these children, however good they are or hard they try. . . . Maybe he likes children?" We make eyes at each other: Think again, aunty.

From the word *children* comes the word *wife*, and then silence falls. It lasts until a friend of the Music Master's from his home city of Bangalore brings us the story. As a youth Mr. Murthy elopes with a beautiful and wealthy older woman from a royal family who becomes not only his patroness but his passionately loved wife. "It's the music in her," he keeps saying, dazzled. "Everything else is an added blessing, but this, *this*. . . ." Others start to comment about karma; about his tempting fate by speaking of his happiness; for gradually and inexorably, the music in her gets swallowed by madness. She has been hospitalized for years now. He never talks of her, the friend says, or of anything else that has meaning for him. He cannot bear to sing, he cannot bear to stop. He sings and he teaches, the Music Master, he teaches and he sings.

A year later Mr. Murthy leaves Madras and our lessons come to an end. So do his concerts and radio recitals. A few records remain, but they are old and scratchy. No one knows where he has gone.

Curve of the Mind

Chennai

Dealing with the spaces that surround intelligence (or what is presumed to be intelligence) begins sometimes with a particular local school we went to; and eventually goes on from there to those inane media questions about finding intelligent life in the universe. To which you find yourself wondering wryly: "How will they *know?*" Never mind empirical evidence, it's another version of Dorothy Parker's response to news that Coolidge is dead: "How can they tell?"

Against stupidity, Schiller says, *the very gods/Themselves contend in vain.* Which takes us right back to all those questions at the beginning, common to many, of trying to adjust to a terrible school: of minds measured against improbable rules of misconception, preconception and general irrelevance. (This against the perspective of education being such a luxury for some of us that in complaining you join the ranks of spoiled brats whose agonies dwindle to petulances.) The school I go to has a monthly ranking system where, if you are ill and miss a test, you are not allowed a make-up exam and merely given a zero instead, so that your "rank" in class rises and dips according to your physical well-being. We're given the hokey prestige value of a learning that only proceeds to undercut it.

I am not yet nine, and have already begun to menstruate. My mother prepares me for it earlier, though I meet her disclosures with total incredulity.

"All women?"

"Yes."

"Everywhere?"

"Yes."

I cast my mind to the farthest place I can think of. "Even in London?"

"Yes."

Everywhere. Pygmies in Africa, bushwomen in Australia, Eskimos in that cold. I have the facts then; I don't know about the possibility of pain. The pain that turns my fingers blue and cannot be eased in any way, because I only throw up the pills along with everything else. Banging my head against the wall, I tell my mother: God must be a *he*, because he certainly didn't know his business when he thought this one up.

She holds my head when I vomit. "And other things too," I remember darkly when I stop, ranging over innumerable and unknown disasters and illnesses. I am learning vocabulary. Functional, not organic, she'll grow out of it. I don't. Not for a long, long time, and not quite. The name of my school, a girls' school, which means "The Compassion of Learning," and marks you with a zero when you are forced to be absent. And with the vocabulary, between head-bangings on the wall, comes a fundamental arithmetic: more than a third of your life. Even those women in London, going to work, more than a third of their lives may well be marked zero in ways I know nothing about.

But for me, here and now, this is only one instance out of a general malaise of unfitness—one's own smallness and inadequacy against stentorian opinion, which will not let you see what you do see, what you must see. For it leaves you feeling, when you look at your plummeting report card at the end of the month, that your mind is of no use, of no account—to such an extent that you wonder whether it exists at all. My mother says very simply: "Part of your trouble is not that you're stupid, but that you aren't stupid enough to take what's laid out there."

And I, pubescent and impossible, dismiss that indulgently as mother-love. Amma, who has been wisest of anyone I know in allowing space for growth, for growing into what you could be, what you need to be, at a particular moment. Very much later, when I ask her, she tells me that's how she has done it, tried taking things moment by moment. And then left them as completely behind. Unlike mine, her mind isn't prey to the emotional backward glance, to all those pointless regrets waiting to pounce. But we share the companionship of regarding "the chatter of the monkey-mind" with equal suspicion.

East—West

The suborning of intelligence at a "creative" level:

Perhaps part of what's called the postcolonial experience, which inevitably gets bigger than that, lies in recognizing a familiar danger at your elbow: the danger of remaining subservient to imposed criteria, whether from inside or outside your country.

On coming to the individualistic West I discover that, as one philosopher puts it: "The personal irresponsibility of the artist here is part of a cultural assignment." It is as if the revolt has already been defined and obeyed. Always with exceptions of course. But to be accountable in your life for what you do in your work seems somehow to be beside the point. No place for a *mensch* in art.

At the other end (past C. P. Snow) scientists in their time of course have been offered a similar holiday from humanity. Oppenheimer saying: "I would have done anything they asked me to." That insidious cultural allowance again: grounds for dismissal by undermining the value of a person engaged in an activity.

Intellect so neatly and socially and professionally apportioned—in East or West—as practical . . . scholastic . . . legal . . . entrepreneurial . . . electronically adept (those bigger and bigger biggies of the corporate mindset) . . . etc. . . . etc. . . . against the deep intelligence required of living. As for fields that purport to deal with "humanities," often enough the misnomer speaks for itself.

To reconceive this inherited edition of the world, to hold yourself humanly accountable, to say: "I'm neither a freak nor a walking privilege just because this happens to be the work I do"—how often do you come across that?

Women artists, among others, can perhaps forge a new voice here. As indeed many have. Having for so long been (and still being, in many cases and many countries) a barrier and a shield so that men can get their work done, and children grow, and life go on, perhaps they can use their knowledge: that exposure of the shield. Not making males of themselves in the process, heaven forbid, and not to discount vulnerability or foibles (a built-in hazard when the ubiquitous in bigotry allows no singulars, and one misstep has immediately become "all women"), but by conjoining their lives to their disciplines, to forge that new voice. Bringing a gender of experience to bear upon work whose shape may willy-nilly be born anew because of its substance and approach—because handed-down forms won't do—but whose essential integrity and integration-of-life must come first.

Sally and I meet in Boston after three years, and drive through the woods into the blue and green and gold of a New Hampshire day . . . delighted every time we get lost, since it ekes out our trip a little longer . . . and talking about these among many other things. Later she writes to me of "the false literary sense we are taught, which says words have no sap, are syllables nailed together as boards. But I believe that each word must exact its breath, is a mysterious partner, spouse, child, prophet of our bodies, our selves—"

Nothing of course to do with D. H. Lawrenciana at one extreme, or at the other the kind of male thinking-from-the-neck-up (or crotch-down) that can reign so fashionably where a preoccupation with techniques can denote certain well-springs of experience unused or run dry. . . . Sally, I know, would summarily dispense with compartments of "social" (as opposed to human) intelligence, designations of "cerebral" as opposed to "emotive." From the vantage of having been endlessly interrupted, like so many of us, but never denying the value of the life she lives and builds, she can speak of fragmentation—the struggle for unity in fragmentation: "Whether it's the fragmentation of war; or between head and heart; or the violence done to the earth, and on the earth."

My sister, my friend, what power of imagination, understanding, and will it takes, to abstract oneself from inherited editions of the world, these laid-down alternatives! Even if we can somehow manage imaginatively, how possible is it to do so humanly, with any effect, momentary or lasting? If *ars longa vita brevis,* who can tell the difference? (Especially when we won't resort to a confessional or defensive wit that perpetuates dislocation? When writing to us, and others like us, is not a game of glibness but an acknowledgement of life—) All we can do is what we are.

A University Town in the Mountains

Otherwise perceptive and intelligent (but finally minor) writers like D. can in some way be/act like ideational children. It seems to show up most when their wives have quality and don't need to parade it. Catch such men by the scruffs of their necks and point them in the direction of a truth . . . okay, even a fractional fact . . . and they will evade it with a deflecting wit that passes for cynicism. It isn't cynicism, for they come off sounding as if they don't know enough to know what they're backing away from. An out, before it has been an in.

Yes indeed, some men have never subscribed to such "norms," while others have begun to change; and their importance lies in sharing an evolution without guarantees. Waters could so easily close over all our heads, men and women alike, in one way or another, in new ways or old, and everything go on as before (as it still does in the vast majority of the world) without a ripple to mar the surface.

You see it over and over again here in academia. The incapacity of the narrowly intelligent to stay with a human subject, to sustain and see it through to the end, unless it is impersonal on the one hand, or bounces off a certain self-centeredness on the other. Lack of a *wholeness* of life + thinking. The bifurcation of roles beyond utility seems to be as deadly for men in one sense as for women in another. Those who have had it easy don't know how to take it hard. Their response is to look away, take refuge in erudition or wit or a camaraderie that serves well enough as a disguise.

To reach beyond that—to discard, to reconstruct, to turn your back on even the relative ease of being laudably labeled "an enemy of the people"—how often do we find this? How valuable then are the risking and active participants of both sexes who try to generate a new way of life. Without them, mouthings become perpetuations. The status remains quo.

Anywhere

The business of reckoning with one's own intelligence:

Where/when does the process begin, and then go on, over how many years and ignorances and struggles to try and retain an uncorrupted mind? Against facility; against the tyrannies of approval and disapproval; against being at times blinded or seduced; more often diffident, stricken with shyness and self-doubt in the face of seemingly unassailable assertions (or assertivenesses) . . . but always with the not-to-be-denied *breathing* need to keep an integrity of movement through life—an integrity of hand, voice, eye, mind—past personal politeness or anger or mistake; past circumstances, cultures and coercions, however subtle or gross.

Delhi

Here in India, the old trip of I-don't-want-my-wife-to-work has long since made a volte-face. No choice. Now a girl's availability for the (middle-class) marriage market—evidenced in those heartbreakingly hilarious matrimonial columns all over the newspapers—depends on whether she is educated and has a job. It can be more than prostitution, it can be the sale of a life: her body for the man and his family's needs, her mind for the family income.

If she doesn't have a degree, to become a clerk somewhere, or if she has the degree but can't get a job, there are other ways of making her contribute to the family exchequer. Karnika is married to a man who is having an affair with his stepmother. They decide he needs a wife to do the housework and bring in some money. Karnika is unemployed, but she has a father. So they force her—beat her—into going to him for extra dowry. For more and more and more until there isn't any left. Then they pour kerosene over her and set fire to her.

Thousands known or never known about. The convenient accidents. The suicides—often self-immolation. In the state of Saurashtra alone (and these are outdated statistics; they have probably worsened since then) 365 suicides—one for every day of the year—by women who can no longer endure the neglect or sadism of husbands, the constant greedy swarming venom of in-laws. Sometimes the throttlings can occur before that. I don't know the percentage of female infanticide in Asia. I do know that my friend Malini, who grew up in the then-princely state of Bikaner, and speaks so vividly of opening her window in the morning to find a long line of camels coming across the horizon, also tells me of the oldest inhabitant in town. She's ninety-something, one-hundred-something, nobody can keep count. Quote: "If a boy is born in our family, I'll climb the two hundred steps to the top of the watchtower, and ring the bell to announce our joy. If it's a girl I'll climb all those same steps and throw her off the battlements."

And we, comparatively more fortunate ones, who haven't been burned or thrown off battlements or driven to suicide, how do we fare?

When an old culture turns over in attempts to change, it can knock its inhabitants off their balance: that slow, perpetual gradient of a time of transition between the old ways and the new. When I become "marriageable," the astrologer inspects my horoscope and concludes disapprovingly: "This character is too strong-minded for a woman." Reviewing the range of all my dithering ineptitudes, I have to hold down my giggles; but am willing for an arranged marriage. Partly because I trust my parents: they will never force me into anything I don't want. Partly because their own marriage, an arranged one, is the happiest I know—and still know, after more years of having lived across erratic bits of the earth. Partly because "dates" are out of the question: well brought-up young girls don't go out unchaperoned until they are engaged. I.e., You can't get engaged to someone until you know him, and you can't get to know him until you are engaged to him.

But I cherish my parents' personal values. They don't preach at us, they just live what they believe, so simply touching the substance of things without ever losing their own complexity; and their responses— never paltry or shoddy—ring humanly clear each time. Whereas I, in my youth and inexperience, know nobody. So who am I to choose from? What criterion can I judge by? Marriage is a gamble in any case, I tell myself, as I accept all this; like the proverbial blind man searching in a dark room for a black cat that isn't there. Cynicism is a bulwark against the sense of no option. Might as well marry the first lamp-post you come across, for I don't think I can differentiate it from some weedy youth in the offing, with a toothbrush moustache and a promising career.

Only when the humiliating process is set into motion . . . being displayed like an animal for slaughter, in this supposedly vegetarian society . . . do I realize that my parents, in going along with traditional ways, however considerately they try to soft-pedal the situation, are trapped too. At night my great-aunt hisses into my ear that the young man in question belongs to a particular sect. Which means nothing to me, so I say nothing. She repeats the fact in syllables of rising significance. It still means nothing to me. Finally, getting a glimmer, I ask: "You mean he isn't a Brahman? But we don't believe in caste." If she weren't afraid of waking the whole household, she would laugh louder. Emerging from behind the end of her sari that she has stuffed into her mouth, she begins to get angry. "You and your parents. Babies! Idealistic babies! Do you know what happened to the last Brahman girl I know who was married into a sect as orthodox as that? They poisoned her."

Civilized, liberal days. Whispered, terrifying nights. When the whole thing falls through, for whatever reason I can't remember now (he probably thinks I'm not good enough for him; and from his family's vantage I'm not supposed to think at all, it isn't my place), the first overwhelming relief is at breakfast: now there will be no cyanide in my coffee.

Boston

With increased emigration among the generation following mine, a young woman in the "marriage market" can face yet another species of hazard, this time abroad. Perhaps a parent or a relative answers or places an ad in one of those matrimonial columns—an expatriate in the land of the free and the home of the brave becoming the most eligible by sole virtue of his relative affluence. The young man may fly into the subcontinent over a two-week break; with luck she might see him alone for a couple of days before the wedding; after which she must fly out and away from all known familiarities to live in utmost intimacy and powerlessness with this stranger in a strange land. She has become a contemporary mail-order bride in a radically foreign idiom.

Sometimes, a lack of the local language compounds her isolation. Sometimes, knowing the language makes no difference. One well-educated bride, locked up here in a Boston basement when her husband goes to work, is rescued by passing pedestrians who hear her cries through the sidewalk grating and call the police. *At least she has cried for help.*

That takes wherewithal: especially given how adverse circumstances (trust Wordsworth to describe Duty as the *daughter* of adversity) are part of the whole spectrum of what is expected of a woman: from a genuine pliancy and affection toward those she loves, to all those obediences—to wifely devotion, to filial devotion, to the good name of the family, to the epic ideals of endlessly noble suffering womanhood, etc., etc., etc. Across oceans and continents, these behests can keep her from confiding even to those who might linguistically speak the same language; for such confidences would be a betrayal of what is held sacred. They would also—given how damnably the victim becomes the culprit—betray her own endless shame and failure.

Today some women's organizations both within the country and abroad seek to understand what it takes even to be able to cry out. They try to provide not only local information and access to help, but also a sympathetic ear in place of lost supports, awareness of a certain curve of the mind. The basic requisite is of course to recognize what keeps an intelligent woman's mouth shut until she can speak.

Mumbai / Delhi

Some personal silences: spaces of, kinds of.

1   Speechlessness after night duty at the hospital, or being at the juggi: this slum colony of migrant weavers from the south trying to stay alive in the alien north. Their laughter on the edge. Their touch on life that survives a far too terrible touch (barely a fingernail-hold) on life. Cannot speak of it; at least, not yet. The inarticulacy of ingestion. The falseness of being a mere witness, finally, no matter what you *do*, aside from giving up your eyelids.

2   Increasingly over the years, some of us seem to grow more and more intolerant of small-talkery, more and more silent in certain predictable circumstances. Leela and I agree that we find ourselves shirking explanations since so much is buried that every sentence takes on the excavating properties of an archaeological dig. Reluctance as a form of social reticence, yes; over-consideration of others, sometimes, when you are hedged about by a thousand scruples; but also a damn-all silence in the face of pointlessness. Of a place from where there's nothing you or anybody else can ever say.

3   That life's-blood denial of not being able to write. Tillie Olsen has said it for all of us.

4   The silences in an innate kinship, loving and companionable, where words happily shrink their outlines and lose their necessity.

5 And then that deepest kind of silence, so qualitatively different from all the rest that I hesitate even to use the same word. To some of us it is a continuum, a wellspring, a base . . . from which we feel exiled, *bullet-holed*, by the needless chatter of everyday. One only has occasional glimpses of THIS silence . . . a vouchsafing of it, almost . . . like spangles of sun on deep water: just a scintilla reflecting the possible whole.

We wordmongers especially seem to be so aware of, and preoccupied by, vocabularies of speech, when these can make no real sense without an equal awareness of the infinite vocabularies of silence—when sometimes only by wresting one out of the other and trying to match them (that kind of living accuracy) can words perhaps be truly born.

Science Lab

In the early 1980s—when notions of evil empires and the factuality of the Cold War are still very much with us—R. from Eastern Europe, so patriotic and involved in her work, comes to the USA not knowing a word of English and within six months is invited to lecture at all the "prestige" universities for being the outstanding expert she is. And perhaps, in the process, to see how other lives can be lived. But how can she act on that? Past all politics, given the mutilation of herself?

From colleagues who punish her for her brains ("So young and she's been out of the country three times already? *And* got an extension on her visa? She must be up to something") to a bestial marriage that punishes her as predictably for her beauty. Against it all, her own fear and entrapment. She dare not divorce the man who flogs and rapes and effectively knocks all sexuality out of her.

She comes from a place where, if you are a safely strictured wife, you can be allowed abroad to do your work and give it the provision it cries for. She comes from a place where, if you are married and have fifteen lovers, it's all right; but if you are divorced and have none, you're a whore.

How can anyone say to her: "Make a personal choice. Don't live with him any more," or illustrate possibilities all around? The things she sees in another country are not within her realities. These things might be happening on the moon.

And throughout, until now, her total isolation. Women can't always talk to each other for sustenance, as they have begun to here, and as we have always done in our own cultures, Sophia and I realize once again, in our kinship and separate foreignness. So many, however brilliant or ignorant, have no vocabulary, no words to say what the world is doing to them.

R.'s choice of survival would take on the size of a defection, that staple of all spy novels of the era . . . when this is one human being struggling to stay alive beyond easy attributes; to retain her own pitilessly attractive body and mind, when she has been murdered of the first and must apologize for the second.

Boulder

Given a cross-cultural spectrum, the single passionate truth of an injustice, whatever its context or cause, overrides local bandwagons and labels, and tends to make you look from afar at groups in general. At the

snuggery of "east coast intellectuals" or "west coast poets" and the like
. . . but most of all at those who develop a melodrama of aesthetics
around which to justify themselves.

This is never to ignore the psychological necessity of groups, in some
cases, or their efficacy, in others; it is only to remember a certain privacy
of the intellect as it affects and is affected by life. For when your space
is so fluid that your perspectives embrace the curve of the earth, it
becomes impossible to abide by any one little pocket of existence. After
all, anyone anywhere must know or comprehend a degree and dimension
of pain, to speak of it with authenticity; the rest is rhetoric.

Places Making People Making Places

NEPAL

Legend and geology say the Kathmandu Valley was once a lake. That fact still keeps you company. Paddy fields are poured into every available inch of what must have then held water—peep over what looks like a ravine, and you see a whole river of rice.

The beaten gold of pagoda roofs gleams like sun on a wave. Eaves of even the meanest houses, huddled together, shelve gently away into the mountain air. Their balconies ripple with carvings intricate as light on running water . . .

The inhabitants of this land seem always to have had such a casual, spendthrift way with their sculpture. Masterpieces like these are often set in crumbling walls, or on struts supporting decrepit roofs. Small stone shrines blossom along the wayside, at the feet of larger stupas; old waterspouts are devised gloriously into crocodiles or creepers or makara snouts—beneath which street urchins shriek and splash, pilgrims piously bathe, and housewives line up to fill their water pots.

Everywhere, everywhere, your eye is caught by the inborn, liquid shape of life in this valley.

Temples

—None of which can alter either the dailiness of hardship or all the irrepressible leaps of imagination and faith.

In the market square in Kathmandu, right in the middle of all the crazy traffic, there is a half-submerged stone in the pavement. Time has worn it to a smooth, lustrous roundness; someone has enclosed it with a brass railing. Dogs who pee on the railing are simply chased away.

"What is this?" I ask a shopkeeper nearby.

"Mandir [temple]," he says.

Just like India.

House of the Living Goddess

Kumari is now all of twelve years old. Like her predecessors, she has been selected from the priestly Gurubacharya community in accordance with her recognition of ritual objects, as well as other esoteric processes that have proved her an incarnated goddess. She lives at the Kumari Ghar (House of the Living Goddess), surrounded by her family, taught by priests, and constantly accessible for public audiences.

On reaching puberty, she must abdicate. Her successor—at age three or four or thereabouts—will take over.

We cross the Kumari Ghar's elaborately sculptured threshold to enter a courtyard overlooked by windows from above. In an instant, the quiet is shattered by a posse of Western tourists led by a nattily dressed Nepali guide, who starts off with an authoritative "No photographs, please." Then he clicks his fingers at the windows. There is nothing in the least deferential about the gesture.

A beautiful, impassive face appears at the upstairs window: high cheekbones, eyes painted long and dark with kajal, a tinsel dot glinting on her forehead. Her scarlet robe slashes an upward glow across her triangular face, answered jauntily by a little red ribbon fastened on the topknot of hair above. She could be twelve or twelve hundred.

But one of the tourists raises a surreptitious camera, and she has vanished in a trice.

An old woman pokes her head out of a side window. A young girl comes tripping down some unseen stairs to approach us with outstretched palm.

"The question is," someone murmurs behind me, "how much to tip a living goddess."

The guide says sharply: "When she leaves this place she will need money to live on."

A man in a red-checked shirt, perspiring, jocular, hung about with binoculars, asks: "No one'll give her a job?"

The guide's patter fails him; his face closes tight, tight.

A woman says on a pitying note: "Will no one marry her either?"

The guide has recovered himself enough to shrug. "Maybe. But who would dare? She is worshipped by the King himself, who is an incarnation of Vishnu, I told you—Can't pray anywhere except at their royal temple and here," he jerks his head at the window, "during the chariot festival. After that, after the King has worshipped the Living Goddess, she is taken around the town in procession. . . ." His voice fades into the sound of these exotic tourists returning to their luxury bus. Someone blows a nose on the street outside. There is a *splatt* as the snot hits the pavement.

The Bhairavnath Temple in Bhadgaon

To reach it, you have to squelch through the mud and straw of a court-yard with a well in the middle of it. A girl is drawing water in a brass vessel. Watching me approach the entrance and hesitate at the absolute darkness within, she puts her pot aside.

"Come with me, bahen-ji [sister]," she says. "I will show you." A firm young grasp encases my wrist as we feel our way up the stairs.

In the shrine, again as always, here as anywhere, it is not so much the flower-decked and vermilion-daubed image that gives you a sense of the place as the layers of human significance brought to it—from the matter-of-fact kinship of this girl now offering me flowers, "Here, sister, take some," to the accumulated residue of living left behind in any place that has been intensely inhabited.

THE BAHAMAS
Arrival

Our destination is a small cay, unmapped and unpretentious, with no electricity or mod cons. From Nassau harbor the ride across the waves has taken about an hour. All of a sudden the boat swings sharply left and heads toward a forbidding stretch of grey coral rock about three miles long. A stone watchtower stands at one end, with a rusty cannon from some old galleon propped at its base and, directly below, a deep narrow cut in the cliffs, invisible until you are almost upon it. Glide through, and you enter a transplanted South Seas lagoon: unimaginably clear water fringed with coconut palms, casuarinas sighing in the breeze, and deep shadowy mangroves stippled like a pointillist's canvas with the gold of evening light. Paths wind upward to the house. A yellow bird flashes past. Underfoot, a sea-shell suddenly develops legs and scuttles off sideways: hermit crab. Here and there, painted figureheads from old ships lean yearningly against tree-trunks, conch shells arranged in clusters at their feet. . . .

Whenever the colonial Englishman is faced with the tropics he seems to revert to a single style of architecture. There it is again, at the top of the path: replica of any number of travellers' bungalows in South India or planters' homes in Malaysia. Deep verandahs edged with wooden pillars holding up a steeply sloping roof (of thatch or tile or tin), high-ceilinged rooms and double-leaved doors to catch the slightest breeze that might leaven the heat, glimmer of kerosene lamps as night begins to fall. On the leeward verandah a long table has been set for supper; on the seaward side, a cliff-edge overlooks huge breakers crashing against the rocks below.

We are quartered in a little hut in a coconut grove to the south of the house. Through palm fronds sifting the sky down, stars hang jeweled and close . . . so close you could almost reach out and scoop up a handful any time . . . in the quick living dark that spells home-touchstone-reckoning, all in one, to anyone from the tropics.

A transistor radio is the cay's main contact with the outside world. At this juncture, on the eve of independence, newscasts seem to be plagued by a pervasive transatlantic schizophrenia. On January 1, headlines alternate the Queen's New Year's Honors List with microscopic details of a parade and ensuing traffic jam outside Miami. Bahamian news takes third place. Local inhabitants put their radios to more immediately personal and practical use instead, sending messages on the air to each other across the islands. "Meet me at Yacht Haven on Friday." "Return home, all is forgiven." "Come to Andros." Or, for all you know, "Get off my foot."

Nassau

Reading about the Bahamas in the Bahamas isn't mere reading. You acquire a dyslexic vision, carrying the compulsion of its slant, to squint past sunbathers and get the view:

The whole long wearisome saga of exploitation is set against a background of bloodshed: beginning with the decimation of the original Lucayan Indians whom someone called "a race of fifteenth-century flower children." Those who hadn't been killed by the cannibal Caribs were seized in thousands by the Spaniards to work and perish in the gold mines of Cuba and Hispaniola. The African slave trade replaced one maltreated population with another; followed by the appallingly cruel era of piracy and buccaneering (far more gory and far less glamorous than Hollywood made out), and then by the throttling of a roller-coaster economy that hurtled alternately down the years from boom (in the heyday of rum- and blockade-running) to depression. Since the 1950s, as is certainly evident during our visit almost twenty years later, the Bahamas have proved a luxurious haven for the dollar and pound of tax evaders—not to mention the avidity of tourist consumers and entrepreneurs from everywhere—while leaving so criminally little for the majority of Bahamians themselves.

We walk down to the waterfront fishmarket. The air is acrid and spangled with sunlight, cutting the edge of manmade things sharply against the sky. Elbows rub, voices haggle, wonderfully pungent smells emanate from everywhere: the marketplace behind, the waterfront before. . . . Many small boats are out, laden with conch shells and bearing at least one fisherman each, who wields his deft knife to disembowel the shells and throw the meat into a salable pile. A whole day's labor must net him the equivalent of a careful tourist's tip. Further down the waterfront, enclosed by pink walls but well within view, stretch the piers and beaches of a luxury hotel. Rows upon rows of bodies are laid out exactly like those fish on the slabs of the marketplace, all courting the sun behind those pink walls that so neatly demarcate the tan of privilege from the dark of prejudice.

Spanish Wells

Off the northern coast of the island of Eleuthera, where the earliest white settlers landed, lies the beautiful and famous (or infamous) smaller island known as Spanish Wells. Its name derives from the rather simple-minded fact that Spanish sailors once found the waters of its wells exceptionally sweet; its fame/infamy derives from its having been, for two centuries, a rabidly racist all-white township that had its own version of the sundown laws. People of color were allowed neither to build nor even spend a night on the island—anyone who missed the last boat was locked up in the warehouse. The inhabitants themselves, descendants of American Loyalists, so jealously guarded their attenuated bloodline that constant intermarriage down the generations seems to have led to an inevitable incidence of stunted growth both physical and mental, or afflictions like polydactylism and locomotor ataxia.

To get there, we take a fat little ferryboat that chugs across from the port of Eleuthera. Moored next to the ferry is a small skiff piled with eggs from a neighboring poultry farm and some local produce, as meager now as it must have been in the days of the original settlers: a few wilted greens, some tired-looking tomatoes. When the owners come into sight it is difficult to decipher their gender. Their clothes block their outlines, Rouault-like, into three upended rectangles. Slowly they walk across the dock and climb in: strange, squat figures, monolithic, impassive. Our ferry starts up; they recede, still immobile, giving the whole lonely waterfront the effect of a painted backdrop. Ahead a storm is brewing. It turns the sea into a length of crinkled grey silk, with a single yacht tilting valiantly against the distant, darkened selvage of the horizon.

Soon Spanish Wells comes into view: an architectural melange clustered around the harbor. Some of the frame houses might have been lifted clear out of a New England village, except that these are built on piles with an open space beneath the floor in which to store firewood. Other houses are of stucco and brick. Still others assault your eyes with what I can only call Florida pink. There are schools, supermarkets, garbage cans painted P.H.D. in large white letters—not a badge of higher education, as it turns out, but merely the initials of the Public Health Department.

After finding our inn, we hire bicycles to ride around the island. Here this is a lyrical experience, consonant with the wind and the waves, if not quite with the islanders we meet. Their speech is strung together with a strange Carolina argot from two centuries ago; under the sun, their preserved white skins have turned not sallow so much as muddy: lightless and reflectionless, as if they had been painted in very flat tempera. In the evenings, when they gather to strum guitars and sing, what emerges is a compendium of sad old "hillbilly" tunes.

Our innkeeper's wife is North American, married to an islander. She has the round irregular profile so charming in a certain kind of woman— bumpy high forehead, tiptilted nose, full mouth, husky voice, all the bounce and vitality that has come down from the Wife of Bath through Doll Tearsheet to the present.

When she begins to talk, she reinforces the lineage into a pun. "I seen all kinds come and go," she says. "There was this doctor. Psychiatrist. He tore up sheets. *Bed*sheets. Yeah. Nice guy. Told us about it right away. 'See, I have this habit of tearing up sheets,' he says. I figured he was joking. Next morning the maid goes in, and sure enough all the sheets are in ribbons. But he paid for all of them. Every one. Very nice man. So *cultured*, y'know what I mean?" And widening her eyes, she flounces out of the room with that special swing of hip and toss of head that tells you that some day, somehow, some Falstaff will find his way to Spanish Wells to die in her arms, babbling of green fields.

Our last glimpse of the island is of people huddled together at what appears to be a school fête. Parents and children stand around in groups, decorous, curiously noiseless. Even the bunting doesn't flap, it flops, limp in the windless air. One of the boys bends down and picks up a stone. If he intended it for us, his aim is bad. It flails across the road in a wide arc and clatters against a pile of doctoral garbage cans.

Departure

On our last evening at the tiny cay where we've been living, someone carts a battery-powered phonograph out onto the verandah. Never mind how tinnily, the first notes of Handel's *Messiah* are flung against the sea and the stars.

But even that magnificence cannot alleviate history or wipe this paradise clean. It is as if here Sartre's *pour-soi* has invaded the *en-soi*. How can the Bahamas be divorced entirely from the ills that have inhabited them? The beauty of the landscape remains a perpetual foil to aberrations, extracting its moiety, if not from your conscience, at least of your awareness. For—excepting a tower here, a plaque there, a church or a flight of steps somewhere else—there is very little human-made evidence of historical memory. The low-flung, innocuous land must become its own object lesson.

In India you can hardly go from New to Old Delhi without passing the Khooni Darwaza, the Gate of Blood, built grimly to commemorate the excesses of a fanatical emperor. In younger Europe the English too try to preserve the monuments of their past; and in youngest America, of course, they can make a tradition of destroying tradition. But in the Bahamas—caught between those two eminences hedging the Atlantic—there never seems to have been the provenance, chance, or affordability for that kind of willed act. And even as I think that, I share a deep and familiar resentment at outsiders' verdicts. Yet I want to come back here another twenty years from now, rejoicing to see the Bahamians claim their own space, their own economic wherewithal, their own way of life, against whatever corporate global nightmare.

At the airport we are besieged by a crowd of lively schoolgirls. "This is nothing," one of them says scornfully, disposing of all the tourist horrors of Nassau and Paradise Island with a wave of her hand. She is a beautiful child: hair pulled back in a pony tail; unexpected, luminously grey eyes; pure lines of face and tilt of head. "This is nothing. You should see Freeport, where I come from. Better than Miami even, I bet."

The crowds are thickening; more flights have been cancelled because of snowstorms in the north. A tall, vividly recognizable Vogue model unfolds herself from a bench. She has a small Bahamian child by the hand. Moving gently together and in silence, they walk to the women's room; the door closes behind them. Two elderly women watch with unwinking interest.

"Touching," says one.

"Bah," says the other.

The flight is called. We board, carrying our hand luggage, our spent holiday, and warnings of the winter storm ahead. The plane circles and dips; the sea spreads out its dazzle beneath, flecked with far beaches, lonely and lasting under the sun.

GREECE
Hydra

Only the Greeks could articulate space in quite this way. The town curves, enfolding an intimate little harbor and then rising, houses upon old white houses, hills upon old rocky hills, to form a magnificent amphitheater: with the sea for performer and the town for audience.

Three years later, in an architect's farmhouse in New Hampshire, I am to discover that no ancient expert ever planned this splendor. The townspeople, in building their houses, merely placed them so that no one's rooftop would obstruct another's view of the sea.

That original perfection of human courtesy carries over into other perfections. For acoustics, Hydra could almost rival Epidaurus. Wherever you are, you can hear everything that's going on—from the occasionally plangent intrusion of off-season tourists arriving by hydrofoil, to the saying of Mass, the tinkle of goat bells, the gossip of neighbors, the braying of donkeys, and the steady footsteps of the cadets in the training school marching around and about, down by the water's edge. . . . Not in a confused overlaid jumble of *noise* but each sound separately: as clear and whole and round as a drop of water. And this in Hydra, literally so dehydrated after being denuded of its trees by the Turks that it suffers a perpetual water shortage.

When it does rain, you want to go out. As I do, in leaky sandals and a minute but even leakier umbrella that about covers my right eyebrow, down the steep cobbled streets that have turned into streams—not to be walked on, merely sloshed through—until forced at last to take shelter in a café huddled beneath the bell-tower of a monastery.

Very dingy this cafe usually looks, when you come in from the bright Aegean sunlight outside. Today, in the patched and streaky grey that surrounds us, it has assumed the warmth of a slapdash family hearth, taking in oldest inhabitants and eccentric tourists alike. The former play cards . . . there's at least one beret to each table . . . and onlookers slouch on windowsills or sit clicking worry beads with their chairs tilted back against the wall. The more involved kibitzers sip their coffee, shuffling the decks and marking scores on a slate that is carefully breathed on and erased after each game. The walls are painted a gamboge yellow, rows of bottles are ranged along the back, and the waiter keeps moving suave and small-moustached between the tables to dispense ouzo and snacks.

The door opens on a gust of spattering raindrops and Edith Sitwell walks in. She must be the oldest foreign inhabitant; her face is an exact replica of the grande dame's last portraits—but there the resemblance ends. This one wears a white cableknit sweater and baggy black pants ending in a pair of blue sneakers, with the whole ensemble surmounted by a leopard-skin turban wound tight around the white hair, throwing her nose into beakier relief. On the way to hang up her coat, she passes us, remarking, "You brought bad weather with you," and on her way back my smart-alecky companion says "We're thinking of leaving it behind," at which she breathes "That's NAUGHTY!" and rolls an Edwardian eye at us.

As the rain courses down the windows and weaker mortals blow on their hands to warm themselves up, *she* orders cold beer. Then she unpacks a paper package and reveals a pink velvet rabbit with a blue bow. "For Sofia," she explains to the laggards at the next table, all of whom raise an eyebrow each and then lower it again. Out comes a pair of nail scissors held in the trembling, undaunted old hands; she snips off the straggly ends of the ribbon, reties it in a smarter bow, and rewraps the package. Then, leaving purse and keys and half-finished beer glass trustingly on the table behind her, she strides off—turbaned head exposed to the rain, bearing her gift to the Greek.

After a while the rain lets up, though down by the harbor the water is still shirred by a drizzle, and the moored boats bob gently up and down. Among them is one we haven't seen before: a perfectly round little boat, so perfectly round that sailing in it must be like going to sea in a cheek.

SPAIN
La Segadera

Even though it is on the Costa del Sol, La Segadera (as I'll call it because of its sickle-shaped bay) manages miraculously to remain a fishing village.

Its unassuming beach, more shale than shingle, has saved it from all but the most fanatical bathers of high summer. Year-round foreign residents at this point consist of a small German colony on the outskirts of town, a French sculptor, and the owners of the inn where I write this, who keep themselves to themselves. "Italians, what else can you expect?" says the tobacconist, slapping a pack of smuggled Trues across the counter. His disapproval extends to the very hostal the Italians own and operate.

This hostal is part of a gracious local hacienda, long since sold. Below runs the ribbon of blue road to Malaga; beyond lies the Mediterranean, with the village itself welling up in pools of white from the dips and hollows of the coast. Above the hostal, too, the estate has been parceled out: into small fields now mown by straw-hatted farmers urging their mule-plows across furrows of wheat; smaller lots where eccentric Englishmen breed dogs; hillsides resplendent with wildflowers in spring; and a rounded green peak above it all, resting like a solace against the sky.

In the course of our month-long stay, we few off-season residents slowly get to know the three co-owners of the hostal. Though Italian by birth, they are part-Spanish, grew up in Morocco, and have now settled here to run this place. Which they seem to do very easily. Carlo is a casual, rather glossy young man with a cleft chin and an American accent when he speaks English. Usually he is perched on the garden wall, swinging an elegantly shod foot, to exchange nonchalances with his girlfriends. Lis, his lovely sister, stands in doorways and laughs. Her husband, Eduardo, is a hoverer. He seems to talk in a series of penultimate sentences and tends to leave and enter rooms at a slant.

Of the three, it is Lis who interests me the most: the spectacular meals she whips up in spectacular bursts of energy; the volumes of Proust and Stendhal she leaves lying open in the living room; her genuine gift for several European languages, so unlike my own linguistic haphazardness. I find myself making up the story of her life—not just common or garden fantasies, but with the detailed pleasure of fiction: taking a holiday from yourself to become somebody else; walking into a fabricated head. I imagine her hanging Caravaggio prints in her room to illustrate the finer points of irony in her upbringing; the metaphors she might use: "Think of me as a Mudejar artifact. Or a page of aljamiado, hybrid as the Spanish language in Arabic script."

But at the end of the few months, I am forced to admit the limits of her repertoire, both culinary and conversational, and realize that the books are only part of a decor. She perches as elegantly as her brother on an old carved chest, and in tones designed for discussing maids, she discusses maids. "Servant trouble everywhere, these days. In Italy! My goodness, you should see Italian maids. First they ask you how many gadgets you have. No gadgets, then higher wages. Imagine! And you have to be so polite. 'Please, if you don't mind, could you dust the bookshelf?' Basta, I couldn't do it!" She shakes her head and swings her foot, face vivid enough to adorn an epigram. "Not like our maids in Morocco. They were so loyal, and worked so hard."

Her being a polyglot makes no difference, alas; she is tedious in all five languages.

Mijas

The journey to Mijas is like saying hello to Greece again: these bare hills, and villages blinding white against the blinding blue of the sea. Agaves and meager trees stand upright in the puddle of their own noonday shadow. Only the red-tile roofs are different, and the flowers everywhere—scarlet geraniums at windows and balconies, bougainvilleas splashing on sun-dazzled whitewash. After Benalmadena the landscape changes, grows more fertile, with terraced valleys and wildflowers brushing the hillside in tones of purple and gold. Fields of poppies appear around every bend, stabbing the grass with an intense red that imprisons the sun in the petals. Woolly backs of sheep grazing. A pig tied to an olive tree, with its snout resting laboriously between its front trotters. And overlooking all this, fincas of apple and olive and peach.

Parts of Mijas are calendar picturesque. We eat lunch (beer, omelettes, salad and bread) in an open white-walled courtyard covered with a grape arbor through which can be glimpsed, piecemeal, snatches of sky and hills, and a tiled rooftop angled sharp and charming in the sun, until you suddenly notice the bared teeth of a TV antenna surmounting it.

So I sit and stare at the courtyard instead. Cacti and ferns droop out of old tin cans painted red or blue or white and nailed to the walls between carriage lamps of wrought (and sometimes overwrought) iron. Beaded curtains hang from every doorway. At the very back there's a canary in a cage. Beneath it, clotheslines drip with wet laundry, and a woman goes in and out, tinkling the beads each time, to tend her ancillary gadget. "The place is so quiet," someone says, "when the washing machine stops."

A bunch of Swedes wanders in, stippled by the shadows of the grape leaves above: two young girls and an older woman, barefoot and casual, with a strained young Spaniard in tow. The tone of their conversation indicates that they are paying, he is being paid.

"No more dinero," the woman says. They ask if he is married, has children, indulgently, as if enquiring of a pet dog about its litter. "Bambino? No bambino. Too young for bambini, eh?" Laughter in which he does not join.

"I have bambini." She points in turn to each girl, then spreading her arms in an expansive gesture that takes in the whole courtyard. "I forty-six. I mamma of you—you—you." A white kitten sits curled beneath a chair to our right. She gets up, barefoot and silent and loving, crouches over the little thing, picks it up, holding it to her breast. "See," as she passes our table. "So sweet." Like the Spaniard. The back of his head stays curly and obdurate while the women begin to chatter all around him.

Suddenly Swedish sounds so much like a Bergman movie that I am convinced they are lightly mouthing profundities at one another about life and love and betrayal beneath our common grapevine.

TAOS, NEW MEXICO

Pre-vision: steep, high inordinate mountains. A plain stretching away beneath them (I didn't know "desert" or "mesa" then, I thought "plains," in the idiom of India), slashed in the distance by the curve of a river. The scale is all forever and forever. . . . The rain walks, designing its own shadow.

When I do eventually get to the place—and on subsequent year-long visits across the span of a decade—I live in a little adobe house that looks like a matchbox made of mud, slightly askew. Sagebrush at the door, Chinese elms shading the west wall, chamisa blooming yellow everywhere. Views of the magnificent Sangre de Cristos on three sides, and the desert stretching away beyond the town on the fourth . . . not sandy and Sahara-like as I'd imagined, but mottled with piñon and slashed in the distance by the Rio Grande gorge. Yes, the "walking rain" of the Pueblo people designs its own shadow. And the power of Taos Mountain presides over it all.

Here, that first time, I live and work for nine months, long enough to give birth to very much more than affection; taking in everything from santos to sopapillas, let alone the people and their land.

The mountains. How they move, seem to breathe: the Picuris rising unaccountably higher on some days, dipping lower on others. Taos Mountain—which hereafter is to visit me in dreams—receding remotely blue and then approaching close enough to touch.

That constant dazzle of clarity in the air, so that things seem to move at the corner of your eye, and you turn quickly and find nothing there. Endless changing dramas of earth and sky; endless shapes and shifts. Clouds. Once a motionless lenticular cigar, ranging across the horizon from north to south, all day long. Sometimes feathers and flecks as delicate as haiku. Another time, such a continuing furrow to the west that I decide fatuously the sky must be thinking. And recognize again how if one needs either the expanse of the sea or the height of mountains, this place has both. Up by the Lawrence ranch, a school of white clouds, dolphin-shaped, comes leaping over Lobo Peak; while in front the desert is an ocean sweeping clear away to the edge of sight, islanded here and there by isolated hills.

One day a storm-cloud cover slams down like a purple lid over Taos, but the setting sun slips below it and turns the slanting rain to gold.

Gold of aspen leaves in autumn: doomed, trembling yellow drops of light against the sky. Very different from the grand old cottonwoods that grow on either side of roads or streams with their branches meeting overhead. Walking under that strong Gothic arch, you think: "Architectonics"—but the word shivers and breaks.

Winter. On full moon nights, even with a million sparkles to each millimeter of snow, the shadows are blocked in so solidly that the world becomes a woodcut. By daylight the Sangre de Cristos seem to have been painted especially by Manet, borrowing the thickened black outline from Japanese prints. Until you get closer and realize that miraculous black line is the profiled silhouette of deciduous trees rimming the ridges.

The sweetness of walking with Louise Ganthiers along the ridge of Des Montes, hugging each other against the cold, and seeing—in the valley far below—fields of snow stitched together with the hoof-prints of cattle and horses; hearing the faint peal of church bells, the scarcely audible tumble of a melting stream.

Discovering, through the seasons here, how fifteen miles can take you from desert to Alpine valleys, where the sky comes *suddenly* down, speared by cypresses, and cattle graze in the meadows. (So soothing sometimes, the back of a cow: the way the light strokes it.)

On the way to Truchas, a morada—squat, grey, windowless—houses the Easter rituals of the penitentes. A single cross stands starkly on the roof, reducing the sky and mountain behind it to mere nudging appurtenances of one another.

Driving along Razorback Ridge you can look, clear across valleys and canyons and mesas and desert, to the blunt and sawed-off top of Pedernales in Abiqui, eighty-odd miles away. Everywhere the surrounding masses of bare red cliffs, craggy, crenellated, bring echoes from across the world—not only Petra but Jaipur as well, those *rose red cities half as old as time.*

Past Chimayo, the road winds between such barrenness to the right and such a lush valley to the left, mile upon mile upon mile, that your right eye gets thirsty for green while your left eye is slaked.

Inevitably, the magnanimity of such a landscape underlines a certain niggardliness of human endeavor. You have to stand up under that sky, come to terms with your own speck-hood . . . as we have to in India. The impulse here is apparently to give up writing or painting or whatever and go for a walk, grow vegetables, or (if you have the funds) build an adobe house instead. Not only every sunrise and sunset, but a casual trick of light, the random part of any day, can be a lesson in humility. How can you begin to convey it all? It takes chutzpah—or the genius of a Georgia O'Keeffe—to answer this landscape with art.

Yet by that very token, Taos can be an ideal setting for an autodidact. Louise tells of how her neighbor, a painter from New York City, moved in more than twenty years ago. Walking past, she complimented him on his view. "View schmiew," the painter said, and went on painting.

On my own door I write on a yellow sheet of paper: "Sorry—working." A cowardly device when you find it difficult to turn anyone away. By the end of my stay, in its witnessing of labor, it has assumed the proportions of a metaphor: faded by the sun, blown by the wind, ripped by the nail on which it hangs.

Parallels

Sitting up late to talk, a native Taoseño says: "You've been coming back now for what? Ten years? Over and over, sometimes for a year at a time. Why?" I tell him I've been smitten with this area right from the beginning—not only for its own incomparable sake but because it reminds me of India.

He throws up his hands. "You too? There was a couple here from Addis Ababa last week. They said it reminded them of Ethiopia. What next, Tierra del Fuego? Timbuktu?"

Maybe. Maybe it is that humbling sky. Maybe it is the adobe, which echoes our mud houses: every roof, wall and window bearing the curve and effort of the human hand. Maybe it's that unmistakable brand of craziness, bringing on a very familiar combination of exasperation and delight. Beneath the archetypes lies a whole range of other possibilities.

As a perpetually erstwhile resident, I am of course an outsider with limited knowledge; as a foreigner, even more so. Yet through each connection with any Anglo or Spanish or Pueblo Indian part of the community, there remains an odd and underlying sense of ease and familiarity. Perhaps—as one Taoseña suggests—I'm so far out, I'm in.

On my first visit I stay for a few days with Edna on Los Pandos Street until I can move into my own place. Edna herself is here in transit, being urban and edgy. At breakfast a horse presents its profile at her living room window, displacing the shrubbery with all the marmoreal calm of some Roman matron. "What are you doing, eating up my scenery?" she demands, scandalized. Unmoved, it continues to offer alternate views of head and rump until dusk. (Which doesn't seem strange to me in the least, given the vantage of a home city where we've had wandering cows ensconced by the side gate, and goats—not at all sacred—perpetually getting their horns stuck through the fence in front.)

Edna it is who introduces me, very new, very green, very naive, to my first Navajo acquaintance, a well-known artist. He walks over and I can't wait to hear the first thing he will say. He says: "Are your eyelashes real?" I say: "Would you like to try pulling them off?" Edna says: "Wisdom of the inscrutable West meets wisdom of the inscrutable East."

At this point the street she lives on is a dirt road. In July rains multiply its potholes. Early morning a truck arrives to grind its way down the length of the street, scattering a layer of topsoil in its wake. It is followed by two men with brooms, smoothing out the surface in tidy dabs. By evening the wind has risen and all the mud is blown out of the potholes. Los Pandos is back where it started.

On my second visit I find the street has been "promoted" to a black-top—for whatever good that does, considering the rest of the roads. Progress has hit beyond repair. Once the town boasted a single traffic light at an intersection; now there are several along the main drag to Santa Fe, and a sudden four-lane highway just long enough to cause endless choking bottlenecks in and out of town. Earlier, Taos had also claimed only one blinking yellow light. You could always give each other casual directions. "Turn left at the blinking light." That too has lost its unique singular. But here as elsewhere the laws of inevitability continue to decree that the moment a road has been surfaced down to one end, it should be ripped up for drains or cables at the other. If this fails you can always count on contingencies. Traffic piles up on the main highway north, where—as *The Taos News* puts it—a cow lay down and died.

On my third visit I confront the visceral: plumbers. My neighbor's toilet being continually stopped up, the sewage line for the three small houses along our lane has to be revamped: pipes dug up, replaced, and shoved back in again. Or so it works in theory. A two-day job. Three at most.

They arrive on Monday: three men, two dogs, one truck, one station wagon and a Cat. By the end of Tuesday they still haven't found the pipes, and our lane looks like a combat zone. The dogs, chained to the truck, howl all the time. Let loose, they attack unsuspecting passersby, have to be chained again, and howl worse than ever. The men consist of an Anglo who wanders in and out, sipping coffee and giving orders; a Hispanic who mutters to me in Spanish that his boss is driving him loco; and a third guy who stands around staring knowledgeably into space. Then it turns out he's there to drive the Cat. Which he does by letting it drive itself while he sits at the wheel with his head turned sideways to look in at our windows. We draw our curtains. My neighbor asks: "What are they doing, aside from leering and peering?"

Well, they have long conversations, and lunch, and more conversations, and a radio that has to be fiddled with until it reaches the right and resounding decibels. But on Wednesday they find the pipes. LOTS of pipes, including the water main, which they burst. Inside our houses we haven't a drop for the rest of the week. Outside, cascades and geysers drown the combat zone. On the weekend a temporary supply comes trickling back in, along with doubts about its contamination by sewage. "Cosily familiar," I repeat to myself like a mantra, "having to boil the drinking water." Each of our three houses is surrounded not only by mountains of dirt but huge impassable trenches filled with slush and still inexorably seeping moisture, until we feel like so many Marianas of the Moated Grange.

The following Monday one of the workmen calls in sick; the other has been despatched to a job at the far end of town. The boss saunters by with his morning cup of coffee, surveys the disastrous terrain, and leaves. Tuesday, when they all come straggling back, I ask for a plank to be laid across my moat so I can get in and out. First they discuss the dimensions of the board required; second, they forget to bring it; third, when at last they remember, the Cat driver absent-mindedly piles earth on it, so they can't find it. Wednesday, with a stroke of genius, they hit the water main AGAIN. We have a replay of the floods, and not a drop to drink, and where's the boss? Off to a town twenty miles away to see his guru.

By now I'm willing to abjure all my old familiarities and antecedents. But when the boss returns at his usual stroll, he wants to know where I'm from. I tell him. He says he has been to South India to study the Tamil language, and asks me in Tamil if I know Tamil. I ask him in Tamil when the hell the job will be finished. He says in English, "I'm sorry, I didn't quite get that."

By the time our lane is finally and supposedly negotiable, mud season is upon us and we residents slither for months across a primeval swamp.

On my first arrival in Taos I meet Dorothy: weaver, superb cook, family therapist, whose loving and generous touch makes all growing things flourish—children, animals, plants. We begin as friends and end as sisters. At this juncture she and Robert have built an adobe house in Talpa, gracious with fruit trees and a vegetable garden. They call it Cold Comfort Farm. "The property tax was a dollar eighty-nine," Robert says. "I wrote saying there must be some mistake. No answer. Wrote again. Still no answer. So I went over to ask. OK, they said, we'll send someone over to take a look. That's just what he did. Got out of his pick-up, stood with his hand on the open door, took a look, and got back in. Don't you want to come in? I said. Nope, he says. This is fine. Got our bill at the end of the month. A dollar eighty-nine."

Predictably, as the years go on, incidents like these are to turn remote and romantic. Richies from Texas and California have started buying up property with no thought of age-old communal responsibilities for the irrigation and upkeep of the land; those locals who do remain strictly avoid the crowded plaza unless they have no choice; the hardware store, where farmers used to stop for a chat, becomes a boutique selling tchotchkes to tourists. Over a decade the town mutates. Life in Taos, never easy, becomes even more difficult. But somewhere in there it retains its own sense of municipal service.

At first I've walked two miles and back to the post office every day to get my mail. When I return a couple of years later there are mailboxes at the end of our lane. What happened? It turns out plans were drawn up for street delivery, and houses had to be numbered. The appointed committee dutifully knocked at each door, asking: "What number would you like?" So now, after a decent interval, we have street corner mailboxes.

In a place like Taos such tales don't even have to bother being apocryphal. A man builds his house out of beer cans, a doughty realtor rides her donkey backward, so what else is new? On summer evenings Dorothy and I sometimes drive out into the desert, right into rattlesnake country, under that walking rain tinged at sunset with tones of rose and gold and lavender, to visit our friend Vicky. From those earliest visits, and over the changing years, we have admired the tables and doors she carves, the canvases that make her the successful painter she is, the animals she tends, the miniature horses she breeds, the stories she tells, absolutely deadpan, in her sweet, high, vulnerable child's voice.

At one point Vicky is married into a whole family of eccentrics who have been living in New Mexico for generations. Her deaf father-in-law is allergic to hearing-aid salesmen; he runs them off his property with a shotgun. Her mother-in-law sends a frantic SOS about Paracletes stampeding the front yard. By the time Vicky rushes over, the stampeding parakeets have vanished over the horizon. Then there's her uncle-by-marriage, ninety years old, who insists on driving his 1938 Ford at 5 mph in the middle of the road. If anyone objects, he points to the dividing line in the center. "See that? Got to stay on it. Tells me where I'm going."

One night he calls just as they are sitting down to supper. "Come help get my car out of the ditch." No, don't worry, he isn't hurt. Yes, he's right here in Taos. Across from the County Hospital. No, he didn't have to go in. No, nothing wrong with him. He just happened to be driving past.

"But that's the safest place in town! No traffic, lots of room. What *happened?*"

Uncle shifts his tobacco from one cheek to the other and delivers judgment. "The road just quit."

Anecdotes can sound like condescending caricatures, whereas the quirk and human enterprise of this place is the space it allows for cranks and individuals in all the three cultures that converge here. Having been born in India, Vicky shares variegated backgrounds and the laughter that can run through all fabrics of faith without deriding them. Her then-husband belongs to a church that sounds very recognizable to those of us who take miracles for granted.

There's the woman on whose face stigmata appeared, from whose palms oil flowed. "Oh yes, and they levitate too," Vicky says. "I've seen them. Boys trembling off the backs of pews right out the windows. Once the whole congregation was writhing on the floor and speaking in tongues. The only two still upright were me at one end of the church

and the priest at the other. I didn't know what to do, so I waved sheep-
ishly at him. He waved back."

Christmas Eve at the Pueblo

The Pueblo Indians observe the first three weeks of December as the
Quiet Time, when Earth should not be disturbed; reminding me of Earth
Day in India's Orissa State, when Earth has her menstrual period and
must not be sown or tilled or walked on with shod feet; when girls
entering puberty are given gifts and showered with flowers, to celebrate
the sharing of their womanhood with their Mother. (At which, even as
I honor that connection, another part of me has to put on its skepticals,
as my stepson would say, and wonder whether throwing flowers sometimes isn't the equivalent of throwing dust . . . in the eyes of so much
want and usage and human waste in so many of our women's lives.)

As Christmas draws nearer, there is another echo. Being in Taos now
is like being at home for Divali, the Festival of Lights. There we float
cotton wicks in shallow earthenware saucers of oil and light them at
night: millions of live, lambent flames pricking out the darkness with
the line of each roof and wall and windowsill. Here the same effect is
achieved on a larger scale with farolitos: brown paper bags weighted
down with sand and lighted in the center with a single candle.

Thus illuminated, the little church at the pueblo is more than ever
exquisite. At sundown the Virgin emerges to be carried in procession
around the paths and plazas of the pueblo and then returned to the
church. Never have I seen a procession quite like this one.

First come men shooting off guns. Behind them the torch-bearers, whose torches consist of fifteen-foot lengths of wood tied together and flaming on top. Behind *them*, the elders of the pueblo, chanting in the Tewa dialect. Then the Virgin, borne aloft on devout shoulders under what looks like a Jewish wedding canopy. She is followed by the ladies of the pueblo, singing hymns. We, the ragtag and bobtail, bring up the rear.

Bonfires have been lit along the route of the procession. Fragrant and finely cut cedar logs placed foursquare (rather like tic-tac-toe in 3D), one above the other. After sunset, as the surounding dwellings—lined with onlookers on their roofs—spring into silhouette against a lavender sky, and the temperature drops, the bonfires are lit. Great leaping roiling flames fill the air with clouds of black smoke, speckled with orange sparks. . . . Through them you can still see the dark, delicate structure of the wood, burning.

Now and again, when a torch goes out, its bearer lifts it off his shoulder and extends it—teetering precariously over the heads of the crowd—to relight the glow at the nearest bonfire. The Virgin slowly returns to the church. The crowds mill and part and mill together again, and firelight plays across faces and voices and hands, and everything is told in flame and shadow.

(Like Gustave Doré's illustration of Dante's *Descent Into Hell*, Henry says.)

Deer Dance

It is held on Christmas Day at the Pueblo. . . . A ritual that says to the deer that have to be hunted: "We know your life is as precious as ours. We know we are both children of the same True Ones. We know that we are all one life on the same Mother Earth, beneath the same sky. But we also know that sometimes one life must give way to another, so that the one great life of all may continue unbroken. So we ask your permission, obtain your consent, to this killing. We will not take more than we need."

This I learn (and paraphrase) later. On Christmas Day I view it fresh, with only the vaguest notion of what is to come. No one has any idea when exactly the dance will start. Indian time, they say. Which is just like *our* Indian time, so I am comfortable with it. We reach the pueblo around 2:30 in the afternoon and wait, standing on a snowdrift piled high and solid on the western end of the plaza. From here I have an unimpeded view, over everybody's heads, of a gibbous moon rising above Taos Mountain in front of me, even as the unset sun warms my back.

After a while—how long? I do not know—I become aware of a long and sinuous line of antlered figures coming slowly . . . slowly . . . over the river, over the land . . . step by crouching step.

Meantime the drums have started to my left, and the inexorable unvarying chant, split by the sudden screams of the hunter-priest-clowns. Faces blackened, feathers about their ears. All the men, the hunters as well as those wearing deer or buffalo heads, and the small furry creatures taken on by little boys, have bare torsos painted brick-red. Just terracotta and not a goose bump in sight, not even in that ten-degree cold. As the animals approach ahead, from beneath the moon, the two Deer Mothers emerge from behind us as if from the westering sun: all in white doeskin; tranced faces, downcast eyes; almost motionless—*still*, even as they dance.

Seldom in my life have I seen anything more moving than that initial meeting of the animals and their mothers, face to face.

After that encounter, everything seems to happen at once. To me, trained as a girl in a classical discipline of dance where each muscle of each eyelid has to convey its appointed moment and meaning, and then yield place—ultimately controlled, ultimately precise—to the logic and linearity of a whole sequence . . . this is another world. No; another seeing of the same world.

The hunters shoot off miniature arrows; the animals keel over, are hoisted on shoulders and hauled away to some place beneath that mountain, beneath that moon; but their numbers never diminish. All the while, the drumming and dancing go on. The Mothers take their minuscule steps; the animals weave and shuffle, bent, in and out, around and around. The hunters shout and leap and dash off, once to roughhouse some drunken disrespectful white man in the audience, then come back to shoot off more arrows.

All those juxtapositions! The uprightness of the women, the crouching of their varied offspring; that implacable mother-dignity and those un-bridled hunter-yells. . . .

I am not even quite sure how and when it ends. Suddenly everything has dispersed back to where it came from. Earth. Moon. Mountain. Sky. And a lot of foolish tourists standing around.

Face on Taos Mountain

A neighbor says: "There's a face on the mountain, see?"

Ridges. Bareness above the timberline; patch of trees below. Mass and accent, yes; green-dark and beige. No face. Somewhere in secret behind that peak lies sacred Blue Lake. I see it better unseen.

But at dawn a broadening light on Taos Mountain brings three faces in one: each appearing and disappearing into the next. Maybe an optical illusion. Maybe a shifting Rorschach. Maybe something else.

Face front, the woman: hair center-parted, eyes grieving, dark, dark. Mother of Sorrows perhaps. Then a fat man's slantwise smile, insinuating all the Mithraic comedy and menace of the old Lord of Misrule. No congruence of face to place. A cloud passes over; he's gone. Last, superimposed and pulled away swift as breath, a fleeting and fine-drawn guess—haunt of planes and shadows, sexless print of what's behind a face.

The *Kena Upanishad* asks: "What force directs the mind to ideas? What moves behind intelligence?"

No face speaks in answer; it just offers a hint on a mountain.

OSSABAW ISLAND, GEORGIA

Here's a landscape snatched back from over fifteen years ago, and still set stubbornly in its own amber—as if in tribute both to the island itself and to Eleanor West, who has had the vision to protect its spaces, even if her Ossabaw Island Project with its ecological interdisciplinary concerns no longer exists.

The magic begins right from a boat dock on the Savannah River, and meanders with you past salt marshes and uninhabited Sea Islands. As the wake from the boat washes along the edge of the marshes, the grasses keep fanning out and folding together, so continuously and innerly rhythmic that you could be brushing against the dance of life.

Thirty-five square miles in all, Ossabaw Island is shaped like the human heart—made up of sand dunes and beaches, forests and marshes—with water for blood and the tide for its pulse. As we approach, an incomparable painters' light slants into gold. Dolphins are leaping around the harbor. A snowy egret stands on one leg. On land, two feral donkeys pose motionless at the edge of a field. A troop of wild turkeys squawks across the road; a snouty wild pig rootles into the undergrowth.

The trees here are dwarf palmetto, cabbage palms, pine, hickory and dogwood, but mainly superb old live oaks with their sculptured trunks. When Spanish moss hangs from their branches, and light glistens through, and animals appear, wondrous and fleeting amidst it all, the whole effect is of tapestry. *Living* tapestry. The first day I go to my room, a doe and her fawn are gently cropping the grass just outside my window, barely six feet away, quite undisturbed. The small deer on the island remind me of the spotted chital in India, though of course here only the fawns have white spots. On the last day, before I leave, there's another deer stepping through the grass outside the window. This one has a tendril of Spanish moss hanging from its right antler, perfectly nonchalant, like a lady in a crazy hat.

It seems to fit right into the island's historical inhabitants, both human and animal. Spanish pirates have used Ossabaw as a hideout, their tame pigs breeding with local wild boar to result in the long-snouted wild pigs that now run riot all over the place. The pirates also bequeath pieces of guns, belt-buckles, doubloons. Original Native Americans have left behind arrowheads and pots of coiled clay decorated with stenciled patterns. Late one evening I walk toward their oyster-shell midden, and it's like slamming into a sudden dark wall of pain. Later I learn that after a Spanish missionary settlement of the island, the tribes were part of a massacre in 1597; by the seventeenth century, after an English take-over, they were sold as slaves. One Englishman, however, who owned the island in the eighteenth century and found it an unwieldy possession, returned it to the Indians, whose "hunting island" it remained until the nineteenth century, when it was sold and farmed. The present buildings—three clusters of them—stand on the site of those plantations, which are said to have produced indigo, rice and corn, and then the long-stapled Sea Island cotton. Following the Civil War, I'm told, Ossabaw went back to being a hunting preserve, sometimes neglected, sometimes lumbered, usually poached.

In the 1920s Eleanor West's parents buy the island. When her son is ten, he is given five Sicilian donkeys. By the time he is twenty-four, the donkeys number ninety. Neither the Ossabaw Island Project nor the Department of Animal Behavior at Pennsylvania State University will consider castration. Penn State has been conducting studies of donkey behavior at Ossabaw for many years, since no other large herds of wild donkeys exist in a single specific habitat quite like this one. Castration will ruin not only the donkeys' lives but Penn State's research. As Mrs. West puts it: "If these male donkeys became eunuchs they'd just *stand there*, for God's sake, instead of *behaving*." So vets are imported to perform required vasectomies, and the donkeys continue to behave without drastically increasing their population.

On my ambles around the island I discover they also exhibit very social excretory habits. You come upon the shell of a horshoe crab, neatly upturned, and neatly deposited in it, a pile of donkey turds. They need a receptacle, they find it. If not a horseshoe crab shell, well then, a hubcap. They'll shit into that, one after the other, and nowhere else.

Animals and birds are not the only life-forms to be observed. The island is a paradise for butterflies too. In the space of half an hour, I see five different kinds nameless to me. A flashing delight of very sassy red. Two vermilion with black markings. One lemony yellow as pollen, enough to make you sneeze. Then a pale nervous pair, so jittery they won't sit still. And one so tiny I can scarcely detect it, except as a traditional "flutter-by" in the grass.

A high point of our tenure on Ossabaw comes on the day when most of us at the Project pile into a van and go to a beach about ten miles away on the southeastern part of the island. The track leading there bumps through a forest festooned with Spanish moss: we are driving right into that living tapestry. Animals emerge right and left—not only pigs, turkeys, donkeys, but cattle too, equally feral. And deer, startled and delicate. We are told of a huge Brahma bull on the island, but this isn't his territory. At one point the track is called Hell-Hole Road and turns into a causeway, with salt marshes on one side and a freshwater marsh on the other. Later everyone hangs out the windows looking for alligators, which decline to appear. Hosts and huddles of fiddler crabs, each extending a single huge claw, scuttle across surfaces; what might be a snake-bird or Anhinga dives backward—sort of regressing itself from its long neck downward, until it completely disappears underwater. But no alligators. The causeway is now edged with feathery dog fennel—poisonous, it turns out, so if you break off a sprig and wave mosquitoes away, they stay away. We see masses of a kind of blueberry, here called sparkle-berries because that's what they do in the sun. Though the marshes themselves are composed of many species of grasses, as a newcomer I can only begin to distinguish two: the tall reddish spartina and the shorter blades of juncus—which is the donkeys' staple diet— turning by October to the color of ripe wheat.

The beach, when we reach it, is about half a mile wide at low tide, approximately fifteen miles long, and seems absolutely empty. Fishing boats hazy in the distance; here and there the hump of an island on the horizon; nothing else under the hot blue sky. Then you start to walk, then you start to see. . . .

Toward the south rise fantastically convoluted shapes of whole dead trees, bleached to the smooth silvered satin of driftwood without ever having drifted. This is a forest that has died in the arms of the ocean.

Strewn all along the beach lies a miraculous treasure of sea shells in every color and species: whelk, sea pen, calico crab, moon snail, and so much more. As the waves wash in and out, they delineate traceries of a darker clay on the wet sand. And when the clay dries that entire intricate pattern is repeated in bas-relief underfoot. There are little pathways of worms and crabs devising alphabets more mysterious than any rune or hieroglyph in the sand. The embroidery of bird-claws, individual and collective. Spoor of deer and pig, squirrel and marsh-hare—swift, leaping little paw-prints and then the drag of a scut—as well as enormous impressions of hooves that could have been horses or cattle or Bigfoot itself. The whole empty beach is as layered as a palimpsest. . . .

Way out in the shallows stands a solitary bull, as if waiting for Europa, stolidly impervious to all the shore birds. An ornithologist names these for us and describes how the pelican young can defend themselves by regurgitating their food into hard and hurtful little pellets aimed straight at the unwelcome. Which makes the more vulnerable among us feel rather envious.

The quality of the island is such that even coming away from something as spectacular as South Beach doesn't feel like an anticlimax. Each of the different ecosystems we experience or work with—marshland and forest and sea coast, river and estuary and meadow—carries its own stunning idiom.

Part of the land is very flat. All in horizontals. A strip of tawny salt marshes in the foreground. Beyond it a strip of blue water, with accents of white breakers. Then a strip of distant islands: cloudy trees clumped indiscriminately together on the horizon. And finally a flat wash of sky above. One, two, three, four bands of color, simple and lovely.

And it all stays with you. No matter where, no matter how many years later, you can see it, sense it, smell it, summon it. There it is, the island.

DAVIS, CALIFORNIA

For some of us it takes a kind of chutzpah to carve our "own" small landscape, against the basic (and all too often criminal) ludicrousness of "owning" earth or water or sky. But now for the first time in years I am putting down roots of a sort, and among other things this means at last being in one place long enough to really grow a garden. When we first arrive at this arid patch razed bare by construction I keep standing aghast, trying to envisage what on earth I can do, until a visiting cousin is finally driven to ask: "Are you surveying your acres again?"

The prospect, I tell her, is daunting. Over the next three years we are to continue digging out handfuls of plaster and nails, Roto-tiller or no Roto-tiller. For all the exhilarations of a challenge, trying to get even a beat-up little desert to bloom can be back-breakingly difficult at first—especially when you're learning everything from scratch in a totally new place which happens also to be suffering through a long drought, soon to be followed by seasons of flood. What are commonplaces to locals can descend like thunderclaps of insight or disaster on an ignorant head. I have no pride and ask everybody for help: neighbors, nursery people, brawny friends, plant encyclopedias, even casually encountered gardeners in their front yards who might be willing to stop for a chat, expounding on soil amendments, water tables, xeriscapes and the like. In a burst of sanity I also volunteer at the University Arboretum to get some hands-on knowledge of native plants, drought-resistant species, regional variations, etc.

Then comes the delight of poring over gardening books by wonderful writers. Not heavy-breathing "how-to" experts, but those who understand the simple measure of the human breath in every activity, and give it to us in good prose. Mirabel Osler's *A Gentle Plea for Chaos* is an ally against rigidities—reminding us that in China leaves fallen from a tree were often left in their own untidily significant circle, to reflect the outline of the branches. . . . In *Onward and Upward in the Garden* Katharine S. White talks of how March brings catalogues that mesmerize you into trying out all kinds of improbable schemes. She calls it the season of lists and callow hopefulness. Vita Sackville-West's *Garden Book* shares her planting notes on Chinese jasmine, *Jasminum polyanthum*. Flourishing here in northern California, it has exquisitely shaped leaves, buds of magenta blossoming into white, and an almost overpowering scent. It also has twining and tenacious tendrils that can lead, as she says, to a lot of deadwood in the center and become "plaguey to control." Her advice is to train some strong shoots sideways, away from the main stem—"otherwise we find ourselves with a task like unravelling several miles' worth of mad hanks of string." Often at the end of a day I've felt like a mad hank of string myself, but I love it.

I have come by that love honestly, if late: plants being among the many languages of my parents' closeness. My mother has grown up matter-of-factly with them in the South Indian countryside; my father has learned about them, patient and scrupulous, all the way from city slums to Cambridge University quads to national and international places of government. In our childhood a special birthday occasions the planting of a tree; both Parent and Marent—as we designate them—grow what they can where they can, as my father is transferred from district to district (eighteen times in five years, around the time I was born), and then city to city, where he also heads or works in an honorary capacity on the local branch of the Horticultural Society, taking the time after international conferences to bring in permissible species from other parts of Asia. On his retirement to Pune, they at last grow their "own" garden. In my mind it hovers over our patch here like a composite mirage, summoned at will:

A date palm outside the front gate. Five varieties of mangoes. Three kinds of coconut trees distributed in clumps along the edge of the compound. Two litchi imports originally from China, one of which does better than the other. Breadfruit, sending off root suckers in all directions and refusing to bear. Sandalwood. *Anona squamosa,* courtesy of seeds in bird droppings and growing fine. Guavas. Lemon grass. Pomegranates displaying fruit and flower simultaneously. A barren avocado. Poinsettias growing at the base of the date palm and reaching, one December, almost as high as its top, leaves stippled sharp as blood against the mop-headed green above. A *Cassia javanica* glorious in April and May. A tall and eccentric *Tabibuia rosea* that flowers in deep red as and when it pleases: sometimes once a year, sometimes twice, or only along certain branches, like a dancer waving her arms. And innumerable others, including cuttings garnered from my father's many walks and wanderings, snipped off by what we call his Sneaky Secateurs.

Among those five varieties of mangoes, the dussehri and the Alphonso are perhaps the most remarkable. Growing up in the far south, we don't know dussehris. Seeing depictions in Mughal and Rajasthani miniatures, we've presumed those are stylized renditions of some perfectly conceived Platonic ideal of a mango tree. But there it is in full growth and detail for the first time now. Graceful, endless droop of stems delineated against a cloudy billow of leaves, with the fruit pale and pendant below. Even the little boy who lives upstairs at this juncture, and is usually lively as a leveret, stands still to look. Following each inordinate length of the stems with his enormous eyes, he says: "Those mangoes have l-o-n-g tails."

The Alphonso has yielded such abundant fruit over the years that my father once suggests we perform a puja of thanks to and for it. Nothing elaborate, just a briefly ceremonial awareness of all that attends the cultivation of a tree. Pruning, watering, fertilizing, breaking off dead branches, is as much a part of this puja as chanting a Vedic verse to celebrate the life-giving centrality of the sun: as important to us as it is to every leaf.

My father is gone now; and with change and circumstance, parts of the garden will have to go as well, like the rest of us; but that image and care of growing green continues to hover.

As I scour the area here in my efforts to make this aridity bloom, a nursery person tells me gardening isn't a science but an art. At first (struggling with the convolutions of our drip irrigation system installed by a shyster who has landed us with a lemon), I'm not sure at all. But then possibilities start to surface, usually by mistake. My designs result from making so many mistakes that necessity becomes not just the mother but the grandmother of invention. A patio I put in overheats— some tiles have to be removed—they yield an integrated pattern—a mandala evolves . . . embracing the four directions and giving me a year-long headache. But I decide this is bearable, shuddering away from some of the "professional landscape designs" around, whose regimented do's and don'ts have nothing to do with my purposes.

For me the whole process begins with a bhoomi puja, a private invocation as simple as my father's, asking permission and blessing of this particular patch of earth to live on it, to have the grace to accept its gifts and the strength to withstand its hardships. And also to make adjustments. In the USA you don't speak of your garden, you speak of your "yard"—a unit of measurement. Whatever follows by way of front yards and back yards must in any case take its shape out of need, surroundings and circumstances, not to mention all those mistakes.

On a street where houses in general stand cheek by jowl, the need for privacy evolves naturally into a walled rose-garden in front, with enough shady space beyond to lead gently up toward it. . . . On this gradual slope I opt for the Chinese tallow tree (*Sapium sebiferum*) as well as the Chinese pistache, not only for its autumn color but because its delicate divided leaves resemble those of the neem in India. Botanical nostalgia also prompts me toward a bougainvillea, which dies here, and cannas that rampage.

The human make-up of our neighborhood affirms another implicit plan for the planting. In addition to long-time Californians, we have Taiwanese and Venezuelans living across the street; mainland Chinese to our left; to our right, for two years a Pakistani clan with whom to chatter together in Hindi and Urdu; further down, a young couple from my childhood stomping ground of Tirunelveli who almost keel over from shock when first addressed in Tamil from behind the bush I'm weeding. At one end of our block are my French gardening friend and her American husband; and at the other, two Mexican families who grow the most blissfully beautiful roses. Walking past one day, we hear strains of mariachi music floating from the windows and find a group of young people in front of their house dancing what looks like a combination of a minuet and a Mexican waltz: gravely touching hands, and turning, and bowing to each other under the evening sky.

All this is a further incentive to bring some of the cultures and landscapes inside my skull and behind my eyes to the sustainable plants in this one place. If sacred or heavenly bamboo (*Nandina domestica*) grows in parts of India and is considered auspicious at an entrance in Japan, I plant it in welcome on either side of our front door. Papyrus, with its echoes of Egypt, thrives along the edge of a north wall—which lacks good drainage, so the soil stays moist enough while everything else bakes—until the stalks get too big for their boots and trip us up and have to be kept mercilessly trimmed.

Mistakes and discoveries accompany every step. Entranced by artemisia with its cascading froth of soft and silvery foliage, you can plant it in decorative little corners, turn around, and find it has grown large enough to eat Cincinnati. After some disasters in very hot dry areas, ornamental grasses seem to be the answer instead of flowers or vegetables that invariably burn to a crisp in the over one hundred degrees Fahrenheit of summer afternoons. These grasses even *look* like the water we lack: spraying upward into fountains, or moving in the Delta wind like waves in this inland valley. They can also flop over and play dead when you don't want them to. Some—stipa, for instance—turn out to be so rampant that I spend the next several seasons yanking them out.

Yet when moved to the slope beyond the garden wall, that same cascading froth of artemisia proves a worthy backdrop to the blues and yellows planted there (after much trial and error) to evoke the colors of the Taos Valley in autumn. Aspens and cottonwoods are turning when I'm last there—an incandescent gold that intensifies the blue of the mountains into a deep, drenched purple. The mesa picks up the colors:

chamisa and rabbit brush blossoming yellow everywhere, with fields of wild asters flung between them in flowing scarves of blue and purple across those illimitable distances. . . . That kind of expanse makes you breathe with your whole life. Here, the minor juxtapositions of golden sweet broom and euryops against French lavender, rosemary and blue hibiscus may seem like delusions of all that grandeur; but they try. The blue hibiscus (*Alyogyne hueglii*) may not be a hibiscus at all; but its petals have the magically faint enamel sheen of flowers in illuminated manuscripts.

Lady Murasaki's eleventh-century moon-viewing in *The Tale of Genji* floods my concept of whites along one side of the walled garden—an "Iceberg" rose; the pallor of a potato vine (*Solanum jasminoides*); white tulips, daffodils and ranunculus; snow-in-summer, etc.—flowering in turn against a ground cover of *Lamium maculatum* massed with silvery heart-shaped leaves, and punctuated by the trunks of white birches that have to be babied along in this inhospitable zone. Then the real floods wash it all away, except the birches, to be replaced by sturdy white irises. No more combinations of moon-viewing plants and poetry.

The patio-turned-mandala makes for an open courtyard in the middle of the enclosed garden, and shamelessly mixes more cross-cultural metaphors, even if they're not always decipherable to the glancing eye. A round central bird bath stands on its mound of earth, representing the cosmic dot in Tantra. Its terra cotta continues the color of the patio tiles and evokes Tanagra figurines. Its turquoise merges into Mughal and Persian blues, blending with the lobelias planted as an integral part of the pattern. Lobelias, let's not forget, have been brought north from the southernmost tip of the African continent and named after botanist Mathias de l'Obel, physician to England's James I. ("Why do these colonial types have to keep changing names?" an indignant friend demands.

"Why not find out the original and stick to it?" Why not indeed: except for clumsy tongues and naming a thing to make it yours. Etymology can be a fascinating friend in the garden.)

So can fragrance. One day in early spring when orange blossoms, jasmine, roses and alyssum happen to be showing off all at the same time, our mail lady delivers a package at the door, sniffs luxuriously, and says: "Aromatherapy! I needed that."

In my language we say a dish without spices is like a child without parents. Roses without fragrance fall into the same category. The faintest scent (of violets) belongs here to the "Lady Banks" rose which threatens to take over most of the backyard, including the nearest branches of a cinnamon camphor tree. *Rosa banksiae* is originally a wild rose from the Yunnan province of China. A doughty Brit, surnamed Forrest, finds it while wandering around two hundred years ago in the Lijiang Valley—pictures of the place show it rimmed by odd-shaped smoky blue mountains—and he recruits his collectors from a village called Ulu Ky, where they use the plant as a hedge. I get lured by seeing a photograph of its graceful arching canes in that remote valley: its white petals, seven slender pointed leaflets, and curiously backward curving thorns. A more accessible thornless double variety is brought back from Canton to Kew Gardens in 1807 and (I can *hear* my friend's hackles rising) named after the wife of the director. Our French neighbor, who has been long familiar with this double variety, says its yellow form is cultivated in Europe, while the white I yearn for not only flourishes here but is drought-resistant. So I get it and grow it, tracing its journey from China to Kew Gardens to my neighbor's French childhood to this backyard in California. It's like touching the world when you touch a petal.

Which can happen in more ways than one. A psychotherapist I know of works with deeply traumatized immigrants from Cambodia; as one of the first steps toward stability she arranges to have her clients plant a garden. So many of us know the therapeutic value of getting our hands into the soil. I grow roses for the first time after getting some very bad news from India, about which I can do nothing—except grow roses.

Those in the front garden have to be of a variety that won't bleach or shrivel in the sun. Two identical deep reds are planted at the very entrance to the courtyard, just inside and outside the wall, so they tumble contiguously over it and glow in the same tones against its creamy texture. As you enter, the eye can rest on them for a moment before moving from the range of colors beyond the courtyard to those enclosed within.

That sense of rest and continuity becomes even more necessary when trying to make a relatively small area become a fluid space. And with it comes the familiar business of connecting different aspects of that inner and outer space. During the planting we have coral-colored Indian silk cushions just inside the living room window, visible from the outside. So I grow a coral-colored climber to frame those windows. That the silk will eventually fray or fade, and the roses outlast them, makes no difference. Thinking back on what the nursery person said about gardening being an art and not a science, I realize that sometimes this isn't even a question of color and shape, texture and placement; it moves into a realm of poetry, like finding the linked syllables of a perfect phrase.

Virginia Woolf says in a letter: "After all, what is a perfect phrase? One that can mop up as much truth as it can hold." A kind of visual truth is what I'm after, to celebrate the ephemeral as well as the enduring.

We unprofessional gardeners need that. You don't quite know what you're doing until you see what you've done six years later. If you're lucky.

Cadences of Craft

Mumbai

In this city, some years ago, we get two old pieces of jewelry reset. Calling them "heirlooms" sounds grandiose and misses the point. These are casualties: broken earrings left by a deeply loved great-aunt, and a remnant of her inherited ruby choker—its clasp of three glowing stones set en cabochon—lying discarded and forgotten all these years. Now, trying to hang on to her presence, I want to turn that clasp into a ring.

The work in both pieces is of a traditionally exquisite South Indian design from Mangalore, and very specialized. It can't be taken to any jewelry store. You need a jeweler who knows the original craft and can be trusted not to ruin it in the process of repairing it. One such man still happens to be in this city: belonging to our linguistic community from the southwest Konkan coast, he has migrated northward to settle here like most of his clients in one generation or another.

Does he advertise? No. Does he have a phone? No. Does he bother with even an obligatory shingle outside his door? No. If you want him you have to go looking for him, and if you have to go looking for him he won't make it any easier for you: that's fame. His craft is jewelry, not signboards; and not, God forbid, a "business"—notions of packaging or shop windows or display cases would be *infra dig*. Besides, they cost too much for trivia. In our language he can only be called by his ultimate title of "shetty" or master jeweler, only addressed in the second or third person plural: that's respect.

Up north a sunar, or goldsmith, often has carefully inlaid patterns of deceit and chicanery worked into his profession. Ill-paid as he is, how can he help snatching gold dust where he can? It's almost expected of him. Each measure of gold must be weighed scrupulously before and after it is given to be worked—which is true enough anywhere in the country, but perhaps without the accompaniment of proverbial stories like the one about the sunar who made a nose-ring for his mother out of pure unalloyed gold and then began to pine away. "He could neither eat nor sleep until he got back the metal by cutting off her nose."

However related their craft, our venerable Konkan jeweler can scarcely be considered a southern cousin of the sunar, let alone be spoken of in the same breath. Fifty years ago he arrived up the west coast from Mangalore and eventually set himself up in a little shed, next to an old building, at the end of an alley without a name, leading off from a street that is closed to traffic because it becomes a vegetable market every day. You pick your way past pavement sellers with their piles of greens, vegetables, fruits and the small smelly dried fish known as Bombay Duck, jostled by shoppers all the way until you turn off into his alley.

There, under a tree, is the shed. And in it, at last, the shetty. A gaunt, elderly man with glasses.

He sits by his window at an old dealwood table, flanked on the left by a deafening electric fan that oscillates at whim and must be switched off while manipulating delicate objects, and on the right by a wooden bench set against the wall for customers. This accommodates three if skinny, two if fat. On the wall hang oleographs of gods and goddesses, demonically stiff photographs of forebears, and a couple of calendars. That completes the decor. His two apprentices sit on coir cushions at low desks, close to a cupboard holding most of the tools. When sovereigns or heavy chains need repolishing, one of the boys hauls his equipment out the front door and under the tree.

The shetty himself seems not quite there. First thing, he knocks a diamond off the dealwood table onto my lap. Its owners, on their way out, panic until it is recovered, but he doesn't lose his muddly calm. After their departure he takes his time to "place" us: which family my sister has married into, my father's maternal clan, my mother's maiden name, and the rest of it. Then he thaws, and I realize he hasn't been snobbish, merely verifying our identity. After all, anyone can walk in through that open door. ("Old man," my sister murmurs, "live long.") What I took to be his senile front is not part of the elaborate lack of front, either. He just won't be hurried. Nothing vague about him now, only a smile of great sweetness and dignity, and all the world falling away as soon as he holds a piece of jewelry in his hands.

"When stones are irregular, our work must make up to them." Mumble, mumble. "The flaw of a real thing mustn't be seen as a mistake." He might just as well be talking about himself, or about the dead woman who wore the rubies. Silence. Outside we can hear a high-pitched haggling over cauliflowers. His glasses slide down his nose, his fingers tremble, his conception stays unfalteringly clear. "Show each gem separately yet all of them unified. As natural as possible, that's the thing. No soldering, it will harm the gold hammered over the edge there. . . ." Suddenly he remembers us. "See? The curve of the ring should follow the shape of your hand—show me." I show him. "So. With long thin fingers, it must be narrower here. Like this." His own sketching hands follow the skim of a boat on water. But the metaphor is mine. To him, as he talks, each thing is itself, accommodating its own purpose, the wearer a part of the setting: to be incorporated as subtly as he conceals his art.

Yes, he tries to pass on his discipline to his apprentices. But how can he convey his care and imagination, the inventiveness with which he answers a traditional skill? "Look at your work," I hear him tell one of the boys, on a later visit. "Don't just go and set up a shop somewhere. *Look.*"

A well-fed customer, who takes up most of the bench, says reasonably: "Shetty, he needs a shop. He has to eat, no?" and then the old man turns fierce, rubbing at his frayed collar. "So have I. But this is *work.*"

The way he looks at that work makes you want to look behind and around it.

Whenever he embarks on an expensive setting, as of diamonds, he leaves the stones for safekeeping with the owners and pays a long house call to "build" the piece, as he puts it. Preliminaries get taken care of in his work-shed. A rounded piece of bamboo about ten inches long and two inches in diameter is smoothed to form a holder that can be comfortably grasped for long periods; one end of it is split into four radial segments and wedged with a wax or shellac into which he embeds the ornament, still in its initial stage and agape with holes for the stones. Similar implements might be familiar to diamond setters on New York's

47th Street exchanges. But the shetty has no electric burrs, buffers or blow-torches to aid him. Besides a small spirit-lamp and the bamboo holder, he carries his hand-tools rolled up in a cloth: a clamp, a magnifying glass, a brush, and textured straps of material against which to rub the finished piece to a final gloss.

All these items get stuffed into a sling bag, and so he wanders the streets of Bombay, sometimes getting lost and sometimes catching the wrong bus, since his directions like his bills are written in the Kannada script of the south, which locals can't read.

When he eventually reaches his destination he likes to work sitting on the floor like his apprentices, on a mat at a low table. His requirements now consist of a bowl of water, a towel, and some soapnuts boiled up to a froth; for soapnut (*Sapindus emarginatus*) imparts an incomparably soft sheen to pearls and good jewelry. He therefore first washes and brushes the stones several times in the soapnut liquid to bring out their most eloquent luster; next he selects each according to its individual placement and hair's-breadth difference in size or color; then he minutely scrapes, digs out, molds, shapes, files and scrutinizes every fraction of the gold, positioning and repositioning every stone to his satisfaction until all have been perfectly set; after which he can dislodge the ornament from its surrounding wax, only to scrape and file and scrutinize all over again, before finally setting up a vigorous session with his polishing straps. For six hours at a time he works his delicate miracles, stopping only for a smoke, or a cup of tea, or to stretch his cramped fingers. On discovering I have lived in the United States he says one word: "Machines."

Vocabulary

Conversations with the shetty are a perennial reminder of how craft can give birth to language. Anything less than twenty-four carats insults him by its lack of malleability; angry when it won't yield to finesse, he beats it crooked and calls it "gold with worms."

We share the same obscure mother tongue, a dialect of Konkani. Possessing no script, it has given us an oral tradition that is marvelously molten. Definitions like this one, phrases of making and cursing, have been integrated into such commonplace daily usage that by now we live their annotation—from the handwork that begins them, to the customs that subsequently keep modifying them, until the act, the verb, can in the end become truly verbal.

Nouns enter a whole other territory. Over and over again, trying to convey the shetty's skill even in a single area of expertise, like necklaces, I find myself frustrated by the paucities of English. Roget notwithstanding, after a generically descriptive "chain, choker, strand, torque," etc., you come up against that blank which occurs when cultural conditions don't warrant a particular vocabulary. Most of India's many languages have a plethora of different words for a necklace. Some might indicate its social or religious significance, its precise place in a ritual. Others depend on technicalities: the specific gems used or not used at all, the kind of setting, the type of metalwork and the region where it evolved, the length or pattern of a chain, the number of strands it contains, the size/shape/design/purpose of a pendant, and so on.

Talking to the shetty makes me realize all over again how the basic idiom of the craft remains an enduring subtext to skills that have kept their daily, anonymous continuity across every hiccup of history for over five thousand years. Certain words retain these perspectives of past and present. The suffix *mala*, for a necklace, or *saaj* (a corruption of the Sanskrit *sraj*) both mean garlands of flowers. Plucked fresh each morning, flowers continue to decorate a household shrine; woven together into a strand, they adorn a woman's hair or wrist; and the act of garlanding ritually recognizes not only welcome and parting but the central moment of avowal at a wedding or a prayer. Immediately, therefore, *mala* evokes the flowers we use every day as an essential part of ornament and ceremony. Implicitly, the word also returns us to the sources of the natural world which serve as the first inspiration for decorative design.

Plants spill their images: grass-blades, petals, a calyx or a kernel (our "mango pattern" eventually merging into paisleys), the juncture of a leaf to its stem, a stem to its branch. Tribal ornaments and creation myths across India still keep their finger on this old pulse. For some on the northeast frontier, the first toolmaker fashions beads in the beginning and persuades a woodpecker to cut holes in them. The Buddhist Singhpos describe their original craftsman searching for iron, in turn asking the trees and grasses, wild animals and water. Finally, when he succeeds, he makes "a hammer by looking at an elephant's foot, and pincers when he is gripped by a crab."

In time, then, here as elsewhere in the world, wires come to mimic twisted grass; soldered metal makes seeds or fruits; sheaves of grain find their way into bracelets; and earrings range in shape from "a pea to a scorpion." Watching the shetty at work sends me scurrying to find more references and records of this movement from observation to imitation to all the increasingly sophisticated inventions that have engendered the vocabulary of his craft.

But the jewelry, like the history of early Vedic India (beginning about 1500 B.C.E.) suffers a lack of written chronogical accuracy. We have no

Herodotus or Thucydides, no Livy or Tacitus. What we do have is a staggering oral tradition, complete with mnemonic devices to retain its every intricacy. Dates may be fuzzy but masses of data emerge, daily as bread, in each area of life deemed important: from religious and household rituals to social codes to the speculative reaches of Vedantic philosophy. To help memorize this vast material, the famous Indices (500–200 B.C.E.) have compressed it into reference points so telegraphic that at times they attain an almost algebraic mode of expression unparalleled elsewhere. Abstruse as this can get, its general consequences for the heritage seem to be alive and well. Layers packed into a single word in a text extend quite logically to layers packed into a single item of a craft. As skill, decoration, investment and symbol—a propitiation for the gods, a punctuation to the stages of life, or an indication of social identity (wife, scholar, initiate, etc.)—all aspects of jewelry have been meticulously preserved for us, recognizable right down to the factual and lexical present.

The Sanskrit Age, at its most "golden" (dates as usual approximate and conjectural, but ending no later than the fourth century C.E.), adds a plenitude of commentaries about the craft. Classical dramatists like Kalidasa, who will ransack heaven and earth for a metaphor, find plenty in jewelry. And Kautilya's *Arthashastra*—a treatise of political economy, also loosely translatable as collected texts of meaning and usage—provides accounts both compendious and exhaustive.

Earlier, gold has been imported from Egypt, Phoenicia and Mycenae. Now it is found nearer home and within India. Lyrical neologisms appear, for gold as also for ornaments, indicating places of origin and associative gradations of color, texture, sound. "Jambunada," found by the river Jambu, is said to glow like a rose apple (*Syzigium jambo*), whereas "satakhamba"—mined from a mountain of that name—has all the delicacy of rose petals. Apricots also walk into the picture, though I can't pinpoint exactly where, as do evocation and onomatopeia in names of jewels immortalized by poets. A jingling mani-mekhala girdles the waist to conjure birds in the rainy season; and laughter echoes in a later language like a khilkhilo, a child's ornamental rattle filled with silver bells.

Region and Resonance

On the day the shetty finishes the first of our two old pieces, he returns it so perfectly repaired that you can't tell the new parts from the old. When we congratulate him, his face breaks into a slow, reminiscent smile. "Remember the courtroom scene in *The Toy Cart?*" This fourth-century play has a judge asking a woman: "Do you recognize these ornaments?" and her equivocations become affidavits: "What have I been telling you? They may be different though similar. They may be just imitations by a skilled artist." At which the judge embarks on a sententious speech about the skullduggery of jewelers who can copy a thing by seeing it just once.

Today the mimetic can be carried to stagnation in hideous machine-cut and "modern" ornaments catering mainly to displays of affluence. "That crime," the shetty calls it on several levels, ranging from the poverty of the country to the poverty of such craft. Fortunately, however, a great deal of contemporary jewelry continues to be handcrafted—signing itself proudly by its region of origin and excellence.

Mumbai has produced good enameling, but without any illusions about where such work can be found at its best: five hundred miles northeast, in the pink city of Jaipur. Jaipur boasts other lapidary talents.

Stories are still told there of the Roman jeweler Castellani, who restored the Etruscan art of granulating gold surfaces and showed some examples at the London Exhibition of 1872; when one of his pieces, damaged in the enterprise, couldn't be repaired anywhere in Europe, jewelers in Jaipur finally fixed it.

Indian granulation today is perhaps seen at its most perfect in the south. Any Madras goldsmith might replicate one of those Etruscan tortoises in the antiquities section of the Louvre, and in Kerala the art of granulation began with Central Asian gold imported at the start of the Christian era.

A few hundred miles up the coast from Kerala, our shetty won't touch this aspect of his craft, except on special occasions. Not that he can't. He won't. Why?"It's their work, not mine." One of his own creations, gifted to my cousin Jaya, is a double strand of tiny irregular rice-pearls strung through oblongs of hammered gold, a marvel of atonal textures and shapes hoodwinked into symmetry. Having cherished this for years, Jaya is now driven by crises to try and sell it. Reputable jewelers, first in Central India and then in the capital, Delhi, won't touch that either. "This is the best of Mangalore work. Even *we* can't reproduce it. Find your money some other way, don't part with this."

No matter what the regional differences, however, precious stones everywhere in the country retain the same kind of potency they've possessed through history. The *Ratna Sutras* (about 500–200 B.C.) describe the nava-ratna, or nine gems, as the earliest talismanic jewel set in a specific sequence to placate adverse planetary influences. In the last century before Christ, astrology shares these symbols with wisdom and the arts, as personified by the legendary Nine Gems—the nine artists and philosophers—of King Vikramaditya's court. A thousand years later the Mughal emperors, fascinated in their turn, take up the talisman. Today

the shetty's customers regularly order luck with nine-gemmed ornaments, sometimes to beckon good fortune, sometimes to deflect disaster.
One evening a friend of his walks in when he is especially busy to request
a nava-ratna ring for a member of the family. At once the old man stops
working, lifts up his head as if listening for something. Then he asks
gently: "Is everything well at home?"

In the months that follow, as we become friends as well as clients, I
begin to understand even more deeply—through his work and my research into it—how our jewelry can evoke the resonance and development of an entire culture. There is of course that constant antiquity of
past flowing into present. Tribal earrings still catch the light, and anklets
sound to every step, in replicas of Bronze Age ornaments unearthed at
more than sixty sites throughout the subcontinent. Quite unknowingly,
our shetty's fish motifs and eight-petalled lotuses have echoed chalco-
lithic findings of over five thousand years ago from the Indus Valley
civilization at Mohenjo Daro and Harappa. And the black and gold of
my own marriage-necklace, I discover, mirrors one of their many designs. Oddly enough, nose ornaments (which have been found here)
disappear entirely from most sculptures, frescoes and literary references
in India, all the way from Vedic times until well after the Muslim invasions of the eleventh century. What happened in between to account
for this hiatus? You can only hazard guesses about fashion, or chalk it
all down to the common cold. Clearly, by the time we get to the sunar
who cut off his mother's nose, such ornaments have been long enough
in evidence to pass into proverb.

Jewelry has also continued to walk, down the centuries, into pre-
scribed rituals and rites of passage: from the first earrings made for some
infants on the twelfth or "naming" day after their birth . . . to the pavitra,
or sanctified ring (at which the shetty excels), wriggling on the finger

of a restive boy during his initiation ceremony . . . to the plethora of wedding necklaces everywhere . . . and finally to the moment during the last rites of death when a body is ceremonially divested of all its jewelry, accompanied by the inevitable commentary about worldly dross.

There are also some variations on that last theme. *A Phrenologist among the Todas* by William Marshall, published in 1873, remarks on the funerary rites of the Todas. An indigenous tribe of the southern Nilgiri Hills, the Todas are said to be Dravidians of Scythian descent, though some credit them with Roman ancestry because, among other things, they wear what looks like a toga and have aquiline profiles. As a phrenologist, Marshall comments on the Toda custom of decking anyone who is seriously ill with all the family jewelry until he/she recovers or passes away, and tells us in triumph of how one invalid proved his relevant skull bumps when he got off his deathbed and insisted on parading around in all his funereal finery until he eventually did die, much to his relatives' relief.

Nationwide, the hold of jewelry and gold on this poor country is staggering. A continuing metaphor, it goes well beyond the metric beats and purposes of the old poets to absorb an essential paradox. On the one hand, the shetty's shed stands in a far-from-fancy neighborhood; he has worked for fifty years by an open window; his apprentices go in and out of an equally open door to polish gold alfresco, under the tree; and none of them has ever been mugged. On the other hand, one study claims that India has the largest concentration of privately hoarded gold in the world. And the identity of the hoarders remains "private": business magnates maybe, wealthy landowners, movie stars, corrupt ministers of state, profiteers and large-scale smugglers of every stripe—some of whom, as a pious act, easily spend millions on gilding a temple-top or decking a deity for a festival.

Yet—that hounding paradox again—the same festival can also produce works of art in sacerdotal jewelry (worn by household gods and humans both) available for a few rupees. Which so many don't have, yet scramble together for reasons impossible to measure in a pocket.

Talking of this, the shetty makes you realize he also serves a hieratic purpose, as do traditional sculptors. "If I want to show a god versed in the ten branches of knowledge, I give him ten heads. It isn't the gold in the pendant that matters, it's the ten heads. Their meaning should be carried to any door that needs them."

In this context—and without condoning any crimes or ills or opiates—you can't think of jewelry here as being exclusively an inutile decoration, an outrage in the face of poverty, or a prerogative of the wealthy. This particular location of jewelry within the culture yields a certain democracy of metals, as of experience. For except during three historically coercive periods, the craft has always been a province of the people, spontaneously expressing their celebration or despair, its symbol more important than its substance. Prayers to cure deafness, for instance, might mean carving a pair of tiny ears in silver—or copper—or brass. However resplendent the corresponding ornaments of the rich, the "baser" metals have never been held too base for this purpose, never at all been considered a slur on the dignity of the craft. What you find at wayside stalls, then, is a matter of human need and painstaking hands, the farthest thing imaginable from the casual gimcrackery of discount stores.

A case of *ars est celare artem*, these seeming trifles do indeed display how true art conceals art, and can sometimes take on the natural, exquisite air of happenstance for which the shetty strives. At the Ganesh festival in Pune I come across molded copper ornaments depicting the elephant-headed god in eight pilgrim centers across the state of Maharashtra. Instead of being "sicklied o'er" with the usual lavish details demanded by tradition, these images of four and five hundred years ago take somersaults in time and place, and come up with the abstract and simplified fluidity of a Brancusi or an Arp.

Women's Rights

At the same festival, watching processions go by, a young couple stands next to me. They have come into town as itinerant labor from Hyderabad, speak Telugu, and live in a makeshift hut near the construction site. Yet the girl wears an exquisite choker as a marriage necklace. Five hand-woven strands of thinnest gold are held together by a clasp shaped like a betel leaf, resting against the gentle hollow at the base of her throat. She tells me it is called a naan, a localized meaning I've never heard before.

"Have you ever 'built' a naan?" I ask the shetty the next time I see him.

"What? That bread from the north?"

"No, no, a marriage necklace—" Multilingual confusion until it is clarified. In Konkani our word for the young woman's "naan" would be "chipput": specifying also the pendant in a marriage necklace. The shetty makes these not only for women in our own linguistic community but sometimes for clients who have heard of his reputation and come looking for him from all over the country. This kind of jewelry is like a regional I.D.: you can tell where his customers are from by looking at their order. From the extreme south comes the tali, as they call it: a carved oblong pendant hung sometimes on interwoven threads of gold and sometimes on a simple cotton strand tinted with the lucky yellow of turmeric. Among Catholics and Syrian Christians in Kerala, the tali incorporates a cross. A leaf-like naan, however, hasn't crossed his path yet.

But women's jewelry is symbolic of much more than the marital state. From the necklaces of itinerant workers, to the earrings of fisherwomen on the west coast, to the splendid chunky silver of the rural north, to the highly differentiated ornaments of householders everywhere— throughout this far from affluent context, the slightest affordable pieces of jewelry have become a habit in both senses of the word, quotidian as clothing. As a young girl I am reminded by my elders "Your neck is bare" if I don't hang something around it. Misguided aesthetic prodding, you'd think. No. Directed at heaven knows how many girls up and down the centuries, such remarks arise compulsively out of some crucial facts about a woman's survival.

More than two thousand years ago, a compilation of laws known as the Code of Manu formulates the continuing concept of jewelry as stri- dhana, or women's wealth. Culturally, many Indians regard this with a sustained note of self-congratulation: look how well and for how long we've recognized and protected our women's property. But boiled down, what does this concept of stridhana actually mean? It means that for nearly two thousand years, until the 1950s (and with a minor loophole or two in the 1920s and 1930s), jewelry is about the only property that can rightfully belong to a woman. And that, according to the Code of Manu, *only* when it is deeded to her within a category of six permissible gifts at her wedding. Widowed, she is divested of all her ornaments. (Technically these may not be divided between her husband's heirs dur- ing her lifetime, never mind about all the permissible categories of arm-twisting which could divest her further.) An unmarried woman, of course, does not exist within these charitable provisions. And all of this comes under the heading of stridhana, or women's wealth.

Laying down the precepts, Manu's Code decrees: *Na strihi svatantrya-ham arati:* "No woman deserves independence." It puts her all her life under the "protection" of men. It equates her generally with goats. It bars her from education. Despite the last stricture, however, some women in the frescoes of the Ajanta Caves, five hundred years later, can be seen wearing pearl equivalents of the yagnopavita, that sacred thread symbolic of initiation into Vedic studies. Now, in the late twentieth century, no matter how otherwise educated a woman may be, she is still not allowed to (and by now doesn't even want to) wear that symbol. For her the initiation rite is still forbidden, as is the beautiful Gayatri mantra taught to males on the occasion, to be repeated every morning as an invocation to life and to sunlight.

A few years ago my father, walking down a quiet street very early in the morning, is stopped by a stranger, a confiding old woman. "I've learned the Gayatri on my own," she tells him. "But since no one would teach me, I don't know whether I am pronouncing it right. Will you tell me where I go wrong?" There they stand against the dawning sun, solemnly repeating the words: two elderly apostates to prayer-turned-prerogative. As she walks away she gives him a decisive little nod. "As soon as I saw your face I knew I could ask you. You'd be Brahman enough to know the mantra exactly, but not Brahman enough to accept senseless rules."

The senseless rules, however, are not only accepted but turn more stringent after their inception in the Code of Manu. At one extreme, laws are laid down about the minimum amount of jewelry required at a daughter's wedding, whether or not her parents can afford it, thus heaping more burdens on female birth. At the other end, learned legal commentaries in the eleventh century squabble over even those six permissible categories of wedding gifts and further prohibit women from inheriting immovable property. Stridhana becomes a complicated branch of Hindu law, applying to Sikhs and Jains as well, and predictably full of conflicting decisions. Precedent by precedent its scope gets whittled away, until about all that remains "safely" synonymous with stridhana is jewelry.

Despite the reforms of the Hindu Succession Act in the 1950s, despite altered circumstances of education, employment and peripherally shifting attitudes, those two thousand years of experience carry their clout. At a friend's wedding I hear someone ask her parents: "And how many ornaments have you put on her body?" Common and sanctioned parlance, this. Niceties forsaken for the sake of survival. The jewelry stands witness, like my father and the old woman under the morning sun, to transpositions and social disguise: of adornment turned into trap or livelihood, of wrongs leading to worse safeguards, and safeguards becoming a sop to conscience. For a sop it still is. Neighbors down our street as well as a leading authority on alankar, or adornment, speak with the same preening magnanimity about how a woman's jewelry is "solely and absolutely her own, which no one may touch." No one, solely and absolutely, except a passing mugger who could yank it off her, a husband and in-laws who could beat it out of her, or the woman herself who feels beholden or coerced into settling family debts. From the epic *Mahabharata* down, a man's gambling losses have rarely precluded his wife's jewelry.

Exceptions, as even the shetty would admit, are no excuse. Yet they do largely and validly exist within the parameters of a culture so varied and deprivations so criminal that any single statement about them must reverberate to a thousand conditional clauses. Against those whose lives don't permit a word like "jewelry" and those whose lives do, only to underline other poverties, there remain many—again, not affluent at all—for whom jewelry is still a durable standby. Legal reforms or no, rural context or urban, this factor manages to hold. A Lambani or Ban-jara gyspy, loaded down with gorgeous armor plates of silver jewelry (she could whack a suspicious character with a heavy kicking anklet or a knuckle-duster of a ring) wears her investments because this is not only customary but practical. Banks or safe-deposit vaults are irrelevant to a nomadic people; and then her ornaments fasten her skirt or fix her veil to her hair with the matter-of-factness of a barrette or a safety pin. At the opposite end of the spectrum, women among the Apa Tani tribes of the northeast border hang safety pins as pendants on their necklaces. And not with any heavy social, economic or cultural implication, either. Some just like 'em.

Men's Jewelry

As for this area of his craft, the shetty says anything made solely for men has become less visible now. These days nobody wants or can afford the flamboyant sarpench that used to adorn a kingly turban, though shepherds in the state of Saurashtra continue to wear some of the same ornaments their women-folk do. In any case, his clientele doesn't extend to left-over royalty or rural preferences across state borders.

Yet over a large part of northern and peninsular India a festival—born not of religious belief but historical trauma—is epitomized by a man's bracelet. Raksha Bandhan occurs on the full moon of the month of Shravan (July–August) and goes back to the medieval invasions of

North India. In the chaos of those times, a woman without a brother adopts one by tying a rakhi, or bracelet, around his wrist. After this a rakhi-brother, even if he has a dozen sisters of his own, must drop everything else and come to her aid if ever she requests it, and sometimes even if she doesn't. Very much part of the chivalric code, songs are still sung about the prince who leaves his fort to fend for itself while he rescues his rakhi-sister from the clutches of a marauding invader. (Which he does by entering her palace disguised as a lady-in-waiting, but that's another story.) "Bandhan" in effect means "bond" and "Raksha" is "protection," though the latter has come to shed its offensive load in this context. Every year now, tying the rakhi and exchanging gifts merely renew a certain reliability of affection on both sides—though I've known a rakhi-brother to travel willingly from one end of the country to escort his rakhi-sister to another.

Days before Raksha Bandhan, wayside shops are bright with bracelets of spangled silver and scarlet and gold, or vivid primary colors as well as Tolkien's "guess of blue." Again these can be bought for a few rupees, and again they are all hand-worked, whether in tinsel or metal, silk thread or silvery wire. Though men are supposed to wear these just for the occasion, many don't seem to be able to let go of them. For days after Raksha Bandhan, bracelets continue to flutter from the dashboards and rear-view mirrors of taxis, the handlebars of bikes and auto-rickshaws, the awning of the cigarette-and-betel-leaf seller at the corner of the street, until the wind finally whips them to pieces.

No, the shetty doesn't make rakhis. He doesn't subscribe to the custom anyway, being southern. But he won't scoff at wayside bracelets either. In fact, this year he has one hanging between his calendars, because it gives him an idea he won't divulge.

Children's Well-Being

One day I find him cursing even though the gold he works has no "worms," and the order—doubtless from one of those private hoarders—is extravagant: to duplicate, in gold, the black silk cord tied around a child's hip to protect it against the evil eye. "Nowadays I'm angry because my hand slips sometimes, and my glasses slip, and I can't see as well as I used to. In the old days I was just angry if I had to do work like this, and called it superstition. Until, quite recently, my sister said to me: "What did we know of weighing machines? When the hip-cord loosened or tightened, we could tell how much thinner or fatter a baby had gotten. It had its uses. Why should *you* have made such a fuss?" So he has mellowed now, he says. After all, children's jewelry has always been designed with a beseeching eye for their growth and survival.

Tiger claws, for some reason, have also been a protective emblem since epic times. In sculptures on temples and stupas, Skanda, the son of Shiva, is sometimes shown wearing a tiger-claw necklace, and so also the Buddha as a child. The shetty tells me his tiger-claw orders have fallen off in the last twenty-five years. He looks blank if you mention wildlife conservation, never having heard of it. He has also spent the first six years of his life in a village at the edge of a jungle, petrified of being carried away by a man-eater. But still he mutters, "Good thing, good thing, poor tigers . . ." as he pulls out an old pendant that was never collected to show us what he can do with a tiger's claw. The most delicate of settings highlights its smoothness and grey-green shifts from opaque to translucent. He has emphasized and extended its outline into a curved, horn-like abstraction with a row of rubies at the broad end and a microscopic gold champak flower at the tip. No vying ornament near it can extinguish its shape.

Putting it away, he says: "This is different. Most things made for children must be *sensible.*" What he's getting at, I decipher after a while, is that past all beliefs and hopes, a child's ornaments must keep to certain basic guidelines. A ring for small children is a rarity, lest they swallow it. Delicate gold or copper bangles called "gole" in our dialect must be patterned extremely smooth, and made adjustable in size to simplify the process of both wearing and growing. Anklets on occasion might be specifically weighted to help an individual gait adjust to gravity or its own structural need. But always, of course, they are crafted very light, to fold gently over the uncertainties of a child's first steps.

Perspectives

The day I've first asked the shetty if I may write about him, promising to withhold his name if he wants me to, he has been wrapping up a completed order, folding the special paper lengthwise, breadthwise, thrice across and across in the jeweler's way. When he's done, he stares at me over his glasses, completely silent. And keeps that silence for two months. At the start of the third, he says: "Just because I work with precious metals, will they think I have a lot of *money*?"

On the whole (with a rare exception or two) his clients may be relatively well-off, but they too are far from wealthy. They scramble, he scrambles. His charges rise only according to the cost of living and are amazingly reasonable, even for a whole month's labor on a ring with a complicated setting of fourteen diamonds. Once I have the temerity to tease him about his snobbery with regard to these patches of carbon, since he sniffs so dismissively at most of them, always using the old names instead of contemporary numbers to define their quality.

"This last order the shetty approves of, eh?" (A third person form of address mitigates familiarity.)

"Blue Jaegers," he says simply. "The finest cut. It's good to work with good things. Been in their family for years—some old earrings they are converting to a ring, like you with your rubies, otherwise they couldn't afford it." Down the street from his shed, pavement dwellers scramble for a patch of asphalt to sleep on. There's no getting away from anything.

We don't meet again until nearly closing time, late one night after the monsoon has ended. (When it rains the alley is flooded, his shed usually closed, marooned beneath its tree.) During his time away he has been told he needs an operation for cataract. The right eye first. "I know the boy who's doing it," he says, referring to the surgeon who is also from the Konkan coast. "He is a good boy."

His apprentices have gone home, the vegetable vendors packed up for the night. Sodden cabbage leaves blow about the gutter; a rising moon like a bit of beaten gold is caught between the branches of the tree. A power outage has doused the street lights and you can see some stars above the pollution. He stands at his door, looking, looking: at the emptied alley, at the moon, at Orion spread-eagled overhead. "They say that signs of the zodiac are the same in other parts of the world? And the gesture of joining palms for prayer? What about jewelry? Sometimes it's also the same?" Not a casual question. Even his smallest gestures follow the careful cadence of his craft.

Dragged back, trying to harness cross-cultural echoes, I think of the anklet on the bronze dancing girl from Mohenjo Daro, and an identical

one in a Minoan fresco at Knossos. Of someone walking around the hills
north of Simla and coming across a shepherdess wearing a brooch of an
ancient Irish design. Of Andromache flinging away her diadem in her
grief, and Schliemann's supposition that it was like the ornament Indian
women wore on their foreheads. Of the Etruscan tortoise and the gold-
smiths of Madras. Of the eight emblems of happy augury in ancient
China, mirroring the favorite motif of our northern jewelry in first-
century Takshasila; and the sumptuary laws in the old backgrounds of
both. Of the jeweled back-to-back Garuda in a southern temple, matching the double-headed eagle of imperial Europe. Trade routes? Collective symbols? Synchronicity? What?

We talk a bit about these and other things. The shetty looks and looks
at all the dailiness around him. Locking up for the night, he says: "It's
my livelihood, they're my eyes. I'm told with modern technology the
surgery can be finished within an afternoon. Not for me." Our footsteps
echo down the empty alley behind us as we walk to the bus stop. "But
the boy says it will be all right. Six months each eye, so maybe a year
then, if all goes well. . . . At least I still have my fingers." And he gives
them a brief downward glance as he goes along, bringing home history
and human substance to the work of a pair of hands.

Dance Story

Chennai

Short legs, long hair, face made up of bones and feelings, so that you never remember what he looks like, only how he is made and how he feels. How, too, he wants you to feel.

You're four and a half years old when you first meet him. There at the dancing school where you have begged to go, despite your terror of strangers, because you have just witnessed your first performance of classical Manipuri dancing, and know now that this is the one thing you have to do.

The north-eastern Manipuri style being rare in the south, Guruji teaches only an occasional group class at the school. For the privilege of including his name on their staff, the school board has provided him with a cottage at the back of the grounds. Here he trains his individual pupils. And from here he emerges to pick those envied "singles" out of the babies' class. . . . Unobtrusively he strolls down to the classroom; unobtrusively he sits in a corner and watches; unobtrusively he makes his choice. If his actions are noted he will fly into one of his much-touted rages. Afterwards you are to realize this legendary temper has been fabricated by the school to protect him from importunate parents. "That is his way," everyone says, as if of an eternal verity.

His way, as far as you're concerned, is as indefinable as a leaf, the sun, the tune of a song. At four and a half, you don't even know you have been picked. "Ao," the man with the shoulder-length hair says. Astoundingly, you're not shy of him. Down you go together to his cottage at the bottom of the compound, with a creeper flowering low over the front door; into a bare sunlit room with a stringed tanpura and the two drums of the tabla, and a single stick of incense in the corner. He reties your ankle bells more firmly and guides your feet to the first syllabic formula: *dhíngtěy-yéngtă-khíttă-dhéntă* . . .

When you have learned both the steps and their matching mudras or hand gestures faultlessly enough so that combining them is no more difficult than walking, he kneels down, face level with yours.

"Now go home and come back to me when you are five years old."

You look at him, uncertain. "That is a long time?"

"Maybe."

"I can't dance until then?"

He looks back at you in silence for a moment and then points to the starry white flowers over the door. "See that vine? It grows from the soil, na? So, dancing grows from the soil of everything you do every day of your life. How you eat," he shows you. "How you pick up something from the floor. How you join palms to greet someone and say 'namasté.' How you move, walk, sit—" matching action to word. "You see? I am dancing. Remember that, practice your dhingte-yengta, and come back to me when you are five years old."

Five.

You arrive, bearing a carved and shining bell-metal platter arranged with marigolds, a heap of rice grains, token silver coins, betel leaves, half a coconut and a twisted yellow bit of turmeric root. Proffer it to him, and bend to touch his feet as a worshipful student should. He blesses you gently enough, but when you straighten up, his tone is sharper than you will ever hear it. "Never do that to me again until you have learned everything you have to learn from me, and it is time for you to leave—understand?"

The early years. Graduating slowly past the first simple syllables to the start of more complicated measures of rhythm: *Kokilpriya, Pancham-swari, Brahmatal, Vishnutal.* . . . The evenings when you badger him to spice the lessons with some drama and danger. "Please, Guruji, show me the demon dance."

"No, *chal*—go—it will frighten you."

"Please, Guruji, just once. I won't be scared. I promise I won't be scared."

His one fault, everyone says, is his tenderness toward children (which of course every child knows and exploits): it breaks into the sternness and stringency required of a teacher. "Achcha," he gives in, and turns into a demon.

Horrible mask-face hovering over outspread talons, eyebrows flared terrifyingly over bloodthirsty eyes, mouth a snarl of fangs, it dances . . . crouch—leap—thud . . . crouch—leap—thud . . . step by step, nearer and nearer.

By the time you fall, panting and dusty, over the fence at the other end of the compound, the demon has disappeared. When you retrace your steps, Guruji is waiting at the window, saying resignedly: "What did I tell you?"

Seven. No more games. Nine. The stage. Which, after the initial nervousness, excitement, blinding lights, and the anticlimax of Guruji picking holes in your performance afterwards, makes no difference at all. There's still milk to be gagged over at breakfast, the same arithmetic to be wrestled with at school.

At twelve, a rebellion. "Guruji, it's not fair! The men can jump and leap about as much as they like. Why do *we* have to keep gliding around so gentle and passive all the time? Why should *their* dances have so much more life?"

"LIFE?" You've never seen him so outraged. He launches off into a spate of his incomprehensible mother tongue before he can recollect himself enough to revert to the Hindi we speak, and point to the same damn creeper over the door.

"See that? Don't just look at it. Fill your eyes, fill your eyes! You think that has no life? Foolish girl! When you can dance the way it moves, you will have achieved something. Not until then. *Sancharini pallavini lata....* Say it." You repeat the Sanskrit quote after him, but grumble in your head that you've just about had enough of being a "swaying blossoming vine."

Shrewdly he shoots a glance at you. "Manipuri dancing must be kept absolutely pure, you hear? No jerks. No wriggles. Not even the needless flutter of a single eyelash. Go home now. I don't want you here unless you can be attentive with your whole self."

Blackmail. Semblances of docility are no use, he'll see right through them. You whip off your ankle bells and storm home. "I'll never go there again. Never!"

Sometime during that week your mother remarks, apropos nothing in particular, that she has been listening to a song in Kannada by the twelfth-century Basavanna. "He says if people see breasts and long hair coming, they call it woman. If it's whiskers and a beard, they call it man. But the spirit that moves between them, travelling from lifetime to lifetime, is neither of the two." Years later you are to see this passage superbly translated in A. K. Ramanujan's *Speaking of Shiva*. Meanwhile, it plays its part in getting you to simmer down and creep back to Guruji the following week.

The lapse of time and manners is completely ignored. He never refers to the episode again; neither do you. After a time it's as if the anger has been both used and used up.

But now he speaks more about Manipuri dancing than he has in all the previous times put together. A little here, a little there, explaining a gesture, a legend, a memory of the green hills of his land, he teaches you:

In Manipur, dancing is charged with faith, the devotional fervor of bhakti. To a Manipuri one's whole life is a dance offering. The Tandava style of men's dancing may be swift and vigorous, the feminine Lasya an apotheosis of grace: fluid movements merging into one another with no clearly defined beginning or end, continuous as the rhythm of birth and death. One style is not more or less than the other, that's not the point. The point is that no extraneous glance or gesture should be allowed to defile the sanctity of your offering. The ignorant call it an expressionless dance. Never! You aspire not to subtract emotion but to absorb it. The true dancer has reached a stage where the earthly audience has ceased to matter, and she is conscious only of the deity in the temple, of—another shrewd look—the gift of life itself.

After all this, by the time you have reached your middle teens, Guruji decides that you are perhaps disciplined enough now to be allowed some-times to compose and choreograph your own dances privately, in the classical mode. If your movements in the Dance of Creation are more vehement than seemly, he looks the other way, biding his time. "I have to let you do this now. It's the only way you will dance right some day. But no public performances of it until I say so."

If, then, you try to check yourself against his standards, there's only the resigned shrug by the window again. "That is how *you* do it. That is not the way it has always been done. Don't expect me to approve. Some day maybe you will put together the old we have and new you have, and dance as you should."

"How can I do that?"

"HOW? You dare to ask me *how?*"

You are silent, but it isn't a quelled-enough silence.

Grudgingly he adds: "Some things cannot be taught, they can only be learned."

Still later, he remarks in passing, "You know the difference between statement and art? Rasa. Simple word: juice. Complicated word: essence. Rasa, the essence and fulfillment of art. An entire world. In dancing—" he quotes again from Sanskrit—"*eye follows hand, hand follows mind, mind follows emotions, emotions follow rasa.* Until you achieve that min-gling, you are nowhere. Enough talk now. Repeat that last section, your left hand went too low."

During your last months at high school, Guruji starts you listen-ing to the songs of northern singing saints—Jnandas, Chandidas, Kabir, Mira. "Theirs is the spirit of bhakti, child, our dancing its body."

Squirm or rebel as you might, against the strength and pliancy of a poetry that can encompass the universe in a couplet, your own personal quirks become somehow irrelevant. Dancing changes, probably grows in you without your knowing it.

The morning after your final matriculation exams, a hot blue April day with mangoes in the market and gul-mohur trees in masses of bloom so red that they *breathe* . . . in . . . out . . . in . . . out . . . Guruji sends for you.

"You did well in the exams? You must be tired. Rest now. Rest. Eat and sleep properly these first two weeks of the holidays. Then we will start again." He lowers his voice. "I will give you the five parengs."

The five parengs. Rarest and most revered of the dances, said to be handed down by Krishna himself, so that a single misstep is tantamount to blasphemy. Outside, the wind rises; a loose strand of the malati creeper, grown lower and more obdurate than ever, scrapes its starry white flowers against the door.

"It's true," Guruji says, smiling. "Shut your mouth, you don't have to say anything. Go home now. Rest. Prepare yourself."

How can you guess what you are preparing yourself for? A year of straining yourself against limits you hadn't even known existed. An unimaginable stretching of yourself, within and without.

Evenings when you weep at your sheer human inadequacy, pulverized with shame at betraying the discipline of this bare room; and Guruji says matter-of-factly: "How can you live an art until you have wept over it? When you come back from the other side of tears, you will dance as you should."

Afterwards you can never recapture the actuality, only sense in the abstract that final fusion: between how Guruji wants you to dance, and how you dance, and how (he tells you later, for you do not know) the audience "sees" you dance: completing with their eyes what you begin with your hands, so that, together, you re-create an art in the inheriting of it.

Bitter Gourd and Green Mango

The Sister

On her fifth birthday, at the turn of the century, she is given her grand-mother's ear ornaments. Forty uncut rubies to the pair: set in hammered gold that curls close as petals around each glowing center, with a row of pearls trembling in a crescent below, to complete the pattern and cover the whole ear.

Maybe it is part of her dowry. I do not know. She in turn gives me one of the pair when I am married; what happened to the other, I do not know either. But in my generation, given the shifting cruelties of ornamentation, we don't have all the requisite holes in our ears, since only the lobes are pierced and the cartilage is left alone. So we turn it into a pendant for a necklace. Involving *links* and *chains*.

Everyone says the new work is not like the old, the rubies not as deep. But I think of her, my great-aunt.

And after my first marriage ends and I have dispensed with a lot of paraphernalia, this one thing stays stubbornly with me. I carry it across continents, sometimes in a brown paper bag on crowded streets; keep it in a filing cabinet under F (to Fool burglars); and wear it, a shared symptom at my throat.

We call her Radha-akka, elided to Radhakka. Our coming into one another's lives follows that covenant as previous and patterned as the heirloom. When she retires as the first woman schoolteacher in a small South Indian town, my mother writes to her. It probably doesn't even have to be said: *You looked after me when I was young, I look after you when you are old.* Radhakka arrives. Skinny, peppery, glasses sliding down her nose as one day mine will too.

With her comes my initial awareness of space around a word: allowance for flexibility, for interpretation, for whole waiting and possible worlds.

Whenever we children have to eat earlier than the grown-ups, she sits down with us to tell us stories . . . and makes a nourishment of story-telling for a long time, if not forever after.

Not for her the traditional legends you might hear from any grand-parent. Her flair for wild stories is topped only by her flair for wilder explanations. She is my earliest mythmaker, my first neologist. Nouns turn into adjectives turn into concepts I never dreamed of, and it is all told in the neuter gender, so that you have to guess *what* is who.

She has one serial about Thitto, Mitto and Apook. (Thitto, by some stretching of vowels and linguistic imagination, could be a very tangy pickle in our dialect; Mitto could be a slangy grain of salt. Apook means nothing whatever.) In any case, Thitto rides a thitto horse, Mitto rides a mitto horse, and Apook rides two horses. Then we have an explanation.

"So they aren't people?"

(Insulted): "What do you think?"

"Thitto isn't a pickle either?"

"It's a *that*."

"Mitto?"

"Another *that*."

"So Apook is two that's?"

"Don't be silly."

Stumped, stupid and prosaic, I hazard: "Sort of Siamese twins?" "What am I TELLING you?" she yells, exasperated. "Forget people and pickles. Apook is double. Twice."

(With the result that I've been smitten with eruptions of Apook-hood ever since, and take to writing no less than two letters or reading no less than two books at a time, embarking on multiple projects and juggling irreconcilable situations even when I know full well that their simultaneity as much as my own mishegoss will doom them to disaster.)

And then there are her tall tales that turn hyperbole into a fine art, all about a rural South Indian Baron Munchausen. Chased by a tiger to the edge of a river, and unable to swim, he shouts: "cooo!" The echo comes back, "cooo!" So he ties one cooo to the other, and swings himself across, hand over hand, to the opposite bank. But he has forgotten tigers can swim. This one is still after him. He has to climb to the safety of a Thumba tree. (Thumba shrubs grow to a height of about six inches above the ground.) The tiger roars, getting closer and closer. He is so terrified, he pees. The tiger comes scrambling up the trickle—Just in time, he stops peeing. The tiger falls back. Dead.

After this we hear about the adventures of the bitter gourd and the green mango, who are brothers, and their sister, who is a squash. She does nothing, she's just classically there: first to be abducted, then to be saved, and to cook for the protagonists between times. The story is told in the *active* voice: A demon who abducts the squash gets vanquished by his own obtuseness. (He hasn't a chance from the moment the rhymes and puns and nonsense words begin—weapons of irreverence against might, which I can't translate adequately, whether into life or English or any other language.) The older brother, Bitter Gourd, is thin and cautious, like Cassius. The younger brother, Green Mango, is roly-poly, inventive, irrepressible—his nature keeps getting the better of his hazards, so of course it is he who devises each victory.

Out of frustrations. Blankets so short that if you pull them up to your chin your feet stick out, and if your feet are covered your top is bare. Appetites so large that you must add a burlap stomach to your own, to match them. Not only heat and cold and greed and danger, but a poke at something else no other stories name for me.

Hers don't either, if it comes to that. She makes me fend for myself. And make a friend of her mythology, so that I can no longer speak of feeling like a vegetable—or, in a rage, call someone a cabbage with academic pretensions—without retracting it at once.

Though she has come to live with us—and then moves with us from south to north—Radhakka won't be superannuated. There is always an accessible if reluctant gaggle of children to be rounded up. . . . And when after my stubborn two-year refusal to be made literate I finally capitulate, she teaches me arithmetic with cowrie shells.

The smallest for units, mediums for tens, larger for hundreds, and unimaginable jeroboams beyond for anything more. Arithmetic with her is tactile and wondrously available. Only in school systems, afterwards, does the dehydration, the dehumanization set in; and I set my face against that. (A friend is to say, decades later, about setting-one's-face-against: "Not a gesture for others, but the deep muscles of the self.")

There is this muscularity in our kinship, hers and mine, since we are opposed as furiously as we share. One day, listening to a classical concert on the radio, I am tapping in time to the rhythm of the tala and miss out on a complicated sequence of beats. "You missed," she says. I hate her. Let me hear, just let me *hear*. Which can't be said to an elder, not even when I want to shout: NEVER MIND ABOUT RHYTHM PATTERNS! *Patterns*. Patterns. I won't have them imposed on me, and have had to absorb them. She won't either, and has had to, much worse.

As a child she is married to a man thrice her age. After the ceremony he returns to his village; on attaining puberty, she will join him. Until then she plays with her siblings—two older brothers, and two younger sisters who have also been duly parcelled off and are awaiting delivery to their appointed roles in life. But nobody can rob them of their childhood. At least, not just yet.

Taken to pay a condolence visit at a neighbor's house, they are seized with giggles and disgrace themselves. The sister next in age is pretty and pampered and used to having her own way. If she can't, she lies down at once wherever she is, spread-eagled flat on her back with her eyes tight shut and her mouth wide open, threatening: "I'm going to die *right now*." After the umpteenth time, Radha eyes her grimly, bends over, and spits into the open mouth.

She is still a child, still waiting to join her husband, when he dies in a cholera epidemic. She joins instead the ranks of "virgin widows" who are beyond any easy counting of cowrie shells. But her father is a social reformer for his time, a wise and good man. He shields her from a shorn head and mourning white, tries to prepare her for what to do next.

Remarriage as well as further education for women are almost unheard of—entailing, if attempted, a whole gamut of reactions from disapproval to ostracism to having stones thrown at you, to undetailed worse. He tells her: "I know you are brave and can think for yourself. If you want to marry again, we'll arrange it. If you want to study, we'll take care of that too. Never mind what people say, we'll stand by you in any case . . . that you are sure of. Do whatever you wish."

Hearing that handed down, I join in the general applause for their courage and staunchness. It isn't until I am grown myself that I realize the issue has been in the form of an either-or, either marriage or education: which is all they are allowed, reformer and unfortunate alike. The choices she is offered are so mutually exclusive that they are gateways to two more social prisons.

She "decides." She opts for education. A degree, a teacher's training certificate. She will not speak of the process involved, only of the end achieved. An earning job, two small rooms of her own in a house around the corner from school.

As long as her father is alive, she goes home for vacations or visits the brother whose wife is her favorite sister-in-law, and then rescues a small niece (my mother) who is in need of care. Afterwards, with the disruptions of change, her holidays have to be spent in the households of other relatives, who make her welcome enough in the gregarious, flexible way of family houses. I can imagine it, that flexibility which can always take her in by assigning her a place as a supernumerary. She is not *part* of the household; she lives alone. Scandalous, but don't say so. Fiercely she clutches at her independence, thereby retreating only further to the fringe. If the bite of her conversation makes them uncomfortable, decorum deems her unworthy of rebuttal, and overlooked anyway in the bustle of their own lives: Poor Thing. In their eyes as in their actions, her chosen aloneness turns to loneliness. She is bitter with relief to be back.

Back to the earning job and the two rooms of her own, around the corner from school. The map of her life, so benignly framed with freedom.

"It was worst for my youngest sister," Radhakka says once, somber.

This youngest one, Sita, is the prettiest of the three sisters, both gentle and physically precocious. She goes off to her husband's house sooner than the pampered middle sister does, so gentle that she is unprepared—for the "facts" of either life or in-laws. Terrified, she starts her mammoth family with twins at thirteen. In her twenties, still so beautiful, she is widowed. Head shaven bare by custom for the shame of outlasting her husband; an inauspicious event wherever she goes.

When I meet her she is rosy-cheeked and placid and loved, the drape of a widow-white sari hiding the grey stubble on her head. Someone tilts the sugar bowl. She lifts it up, wipes its rim, and sets it tenderly back in place. Her gentleness is intact and formidable. Self-generating perhaps—irrespective of its object, or of what the subject has been subjected to. For all their evidence, the predicates are nowhere in sight. I am awed and adoring, like everyone else (you can't resist her); but it is impossible to decipher the sentences of . . . and on . . . her life. They read almost too successfully like what my own sister calls the Sita syndrome—referring to the goddess Sita, who is the epic ideal of noble, suffering womanhood.

But this lovely human Sita has something else besides: laughter. The minute she see Radhakka she remembers the disastrous condolence visit of their childhood and gets the giggles again. "You were always so *sharp*," she says admiringly at one point. "Not like me—" Maybe that's it? In part? Later, with the same loving italicized softness, she remarks to my mother: "You know, Radhakka has never known how to *bend*."

But that is perhaps what I cherish most in Radhakka, though it inevitably makes waves for those around her.

My mother, who has never so far had any "servant trouble" because her every gesture underlines mutuality and allows space, suddenly finds cooks giving notice: "You may have to put up with the old woman because you're related to her. I am not, thank God, so I'm leaving."

And I *am*, thank God (related, not leaving or cooking or running a multifarious household), and I appreciate her.

She shows me ungainliness; difficulties; misfitting; a continuing resentment, even so many years later, at having been made to feel by her own so-different mother like an ugly duckling set in aspic—and this in and from a place where to speak disrespectfully of your dead parents (especially to children) is considered blasphemy.

She's cantankerous, impatient, often so transparently wrong—the first adult I know who makes a present to me of her failings. There they are, as clear as my own. She relieves me of exemplars, and . . . all unwitting . . . allows me to be critical with or without laughter.

—Sometimes she does it on the spot:

Like the rest of us but especially those of her generation, she too is permeated with traditional beliefs and speaks often of "time"—for birth and death and karmic cycles.

One day we are looking over our respective patches of garden. (She grows vegetables, so I grow flowers.) Inadvertently she steps on an antheap, is bitten, and starts in a fury to stamp on every ant in sight, killing them all.

"Radhakka!" I protest. "Radhakka, stop! What are you doing?"

"Their time has come," she says, stamping away.

—Sometimes she does it in retrospect:

After that first week of lessons, her verdict is pronounced, to be repeated at intervals over the years: "With your brains you should have been a boy."

And of course she makes the authoritative statement as meekly as I hear it. We are contemporaries across generations, giving us contemporaries across cultures; what we say to one another doesn't belong to us alone.

Not all her stories are funny or outrageous. In certain anecdotes about her own life, a strangeness creeps in.

During those early vacations spent at her parents' house, she encounters a mendicant yogi on every visit. He comes at dusk, usually when everyone else happens to be away (at places where, as a widow, she cannot go).

"I thought he was begging, and went to the kitchen to get some rice. I was a little frightened—" There's a half-giggle in her voice. Fear? I see the isolation of the house, with only the forest and the fields outside, and darkness gathering at the windows. "So I hesitated. But he only went three times around the house, sprinkling handfuls of water from his pitcher . . . like a purification ceremony, you know? . . . and when I looked again he was gone."

With the rest of her stories, this stays with me. Once I mention it to her younger brother, my favorite great-uncle. He is rather a renaissance man: veterinarian, historian, scientist (whose contributions to research at home and abroad are beyond my fathoming, though I do know of a wriggling microbe somewhere burdened with his resounding twelvesyllabled name because he discovered its existence). He also puts up with my endlessly devouring curiosities. This time I happen to be obsessed with ascetic rituals, and remember Radhakka's yogi.

"What was he doing? Was that Ganges-water to protect your house?"

"Oh, that." He dismisses it. "That was her husband. He was always appearing in different forms and calling her through the window."

He doesn't mean aberrations, he means ghosts.

I flounder, trying to disentangle, understand. Not about ghosts, which are a common enough property, but the effect on *her*.

How does she feel, how did she feel, unclaimed wife of a stranger husband, revenant or otherwise?

Who is claiming what?

I can never ask her. Not out of respect-to-elders, but out of courtesy. This cuts too close; I can't trespass.

There is a time in Radhakka's life of which nobody speaks. Blank. Except for a hint once, when I myself am in my teens, from an aunt of mine who is about the most alive person I know, and to whom I still find myself starting to write letters, more than fifteen years after her death. But she is a generation down, so her knowledge, as she admits, is equally spotty with reticence and hearsay.

Perhaps another lodger in the same house where Radhakka rents her rooms. Perhaps not. She goes away. The family has it that she is ill and needs special treatment, an extended convalescence. Whether it is her body that must be punished for its wanting or her mind that must be safeguarded from hurt, nobody knows. It is all hushed up. Perhaps if "the truth" came out, she would be expelled from the school.

"How *can* they?" I burst out. With this aunt I can be as passionately vociferous as I wish, but even so I'm trained not to mention sex. Or the emotions it engenders. "When I hear Radhakka talk, sometimes, I almost wish something had happened—that is, if it was worth the anguish for her. . . . Oh, but how *can* they? How can a need be treated like a disgrace?"

My aunt looks at me, very silent, very dry. Yet some years later, my mother gets furious in her turn when the topic comes up—"The rubbish people talk!" Her anger arises as much from facts as from loyalty, for she can attest, from having attended Radhakka medically, that she was indeed "a virgin widow" in that pet phrase of orthodoxy, no matter what it was that had or hadn't happened. The blank remains.

Back Radhakka goes, then, after that nameless interval. Back to the two rooms around the corner from school. She becomes intensely religious. The town has an ashram built around the presence of a holy man. The swami is revered; he doesn't have to run around making miracles to prove his saintliness. Any activities attached to the place—from charitable work to communal meals to lectures and discussions—are sanctioned and safe. More and more of her evenings are spent there. (All this is a subterranean understanding between us, and never spelled out: shadows of thatch I have not seen falling on the texture of cotton carpets spread on the floor; and Radhakka sitting there, willing herself to be *still*. . . .) Quiet and the presence of her swami.

"NO ONE like him!" she says pugnaciously, though nobody is about to contradict her. When she comes to us she brings his photograph in a wooden frame and accords it highest honor in our household shrine. All other gods and goddesses make way without protest for this gentle, bespectacled old man who has given her anchor: he is sitting on a chair, wrapped in a shawl; there's a tiger-skin on the floor beneath, and his hanging feet don't . . . quite . . . touch it.

Before she can get "detached" into the desired non-desiring, and long before she comes to stay with us, the independence movement has gathered momentum. There is space carved in it for her, as for anyone irrespective of gender or social stigma. She throws herself in. And here too the guru and the gospel advocate nonviolence.

All the after-years we spend together, I am to see this sundering in her. The passionate political convictions, and that constant nudge at her elbow reminding her to be gentle. The zest for a fight becoming a streak of malice when fisticuffs (even as a metaphor) are taboo.

Yet there's another stubborn zest that won't be stilled. She doesn't lose it until the death of her brother's wife, her best friend and adversary whom she has championed like a cause over the years—a companionship instantly renewed whenever they meet. They insist on reading letters together, but neither will use glasses, and Radhakka is nearsighted and her sister-in-law is farsighted.

"You're holding it too close!"

"You're holding it too far!"

Too close, too far, back and forth, too close, too far, goes the letter until it is nearly in shreds; but they have read it together, like the past.

Now she no longer wants to live. Long, long months and years of slow atrophy. The oxygen tent, the catheter. Hospitals are overcrowded. My mother does it all, beyond covenants; and the rest of us help out as much as we can, I whenever I am home from college, sitting evening after evening at her bedside, trying to wring a laugh out of her sometimes by telling her tales like her own. But when I make an equally sorry job of trying to thank her for the sustenance of those stories, she gives me a polite smile and says vaguely: "What stories?" As she turns her head for a sip of water the lamplight shines translucent through the shell of her ear, and I can see the holes bored in the cartilage for the ornaments the child-bride once wore.

Radhakka's mind is going but it keeps hold of its division, riven down to the last splinters. Sporadically she asks for the newspaper she has always subscribed to, and keeps track of my father's meetings with Nehru about the current Five Year Plan, calling me in to whisper: "Tell him to be sure not to forget *this* aspect. . . ."

"Yes," I soothe her. "Yes, yes."

As I am going out she calls me in again, suddenly sharp. "Also be sure to put the right things in the kurkut, so we'll have no trouble from beyond the river."

"Yes," I say again, but now mere soothing won't do. I respect her reasons even when they are failing her, and this seems more than senility—it matters to her, and I don't know what she's talking about. So I chase all over the house until I find my mother. "Amma, what is a kurkut?"

A niche set in the wall of an ancestral house, it turns out, where votive offerings are deposited and must be kept undisturbed if they are to prove their placation.

"And what was beyond the river?"

A village. A village whose powers of evil are so potent that nobody dares utter its name. It is referred to, under the breath, as Beyond-the-River instead.

One night we do all we can, and almost nothing helps. My mother, *garde-malade*, casts about for ways to make endurable what is clearly more than physical agony. "Do you think you can try to keep your mind on your swami?"

"I can't," Radhakka whispers. "Because he is not there. There's no one there."

Radhakka, Radhakka, you who taught me about telling stories of a sort, perhaps it would be kinder to you, to me, to all of us, if I told this as a story too, but I can't. This is not to patronize our storytelling past, not to disavow respect or need. For yes, after pain that formal feeling comes, and there can be a tale . . . funny or sad, but uninjured by birth . . . that speaks of what happened.

As once you told me of twelfth-century Basavanna, whose songs and sayings you loved, maybe I can mention this century's Cocteau, saying, "Find out what you can do, and then do something else." I don't want to resort to any practiced craft or fabrication to make you "readable." Just get our bare bones out of the pot, and that perhaps sounds too cannibalistic for comfort; but we have all been there, in one way or another, so why pretend and make pretty? I don't want a form of art, I want a form of life, to honor you as your own life never did.

Cessation and Continuity

The Brother

Why does a man decide to marry his dead wife's younger sister?

In my grandfather's case, perhaps partly because the two women look rather alike. He is pressured into remarriage by well-meaning elders trying to yank him out of the terrible state he has fallen into, and from which he seems unable to emerge. He thinks (if he can think), or is advised, that at least keeping it in the family will ensure his children's well-being.

But those children, my mother, the youngest, in particular, are to suffer their stepmother-aunt's unspeakable abuse—literally unspeakable, for it is glossed over by reticence, forbearance and the painful ease of later apology (dribbling chin; old hand clutching the quiet one that is wiping her up: "Forgive me . . . forgive me . . .") across the erasures of children become adults and adults become senile.

And in him, in my grandfather, throughout, the sharp and endless *missing* of his first wife that he lets me see, when he is old and I am growing up, watching it all, wondering. . . .

In those days, as in these days, you probably don't get to know your wife until you marry her. Maybe he is misled by physical hunger and loss to impute too much to a physical resemblance. If so, it can't take him longer than the morning after his second marriage to realize that here what is appeased is annihilated in the same breath. For fifty-three years.

What gives me the authority to say that when I have none?

Even Radhakka, my pipeline to the past, has said only little in her way that says much. "She was so beautiful, your mother's mother. Her back was smooth as butter. I gave her a massage once. . . . I'll never forget." And: "She wrote to me when your mother was born. She said, 'This my youngest is the most exquisite of the three but I feel I will not live to see her grow.' She didn't care that I'd storm at her and tell her not to say such inauspicious things. She had a truth to her. . . . Seeing your grandparents together was like that too. Death can't alter that."

It alters other things. As a civil engineer he becomes known both for his dams and roads and bridges in the mountain jungles of Coorg and also for his almost insane, uncontrollable rages. It is as if he spends the first half of his adult life struggling with the forces outside him and the second half struggling with the forces inside him. By the time he and I get to know each other, he lives surrounded by growing things: plants and children and a quiet that isn't disturbed by noise.

They don't mention my mother's mother, his first wife, in that house

now filled with the second family. For all the evidence of her own prog-
eny, she might never have existed.

Except on evenings when my parents, who live across town, have to
go out and drop me off there (growing girl-children can't be left alone
at home) to be picked up later. Then the old man and I listen to music
on the radio, or walk around to see how the mango trees are bearing;
and he talks.

It isn't merely that his voice changes when he speaks of his first wife;
the very syllables seems different . . . difficult at first, as if contradicted
by speech: sounding from where words cannot. Until *she* comes to clothe
them. Then I see her alive in the silences of his speech, in those spaces,
and in his compunctions.

Hot day. Studying for an exam. Needing to find her in that jumble of
a joint-family home. (He doesn't have to say this; that is how it is.) She
is in the kitchen, cooking over an open earthen fireplace, blowing at the
logs. Sweat streams down her face; she lifts her forearm to wipe it out
of her eyes and push back a strand of hair, leaving a smear of soot across
her forehead.

He wants to get her out of there, out for a walk into the cool of the
path through the trees, wearing her green going-out sari she likes so
much, and with jasmine in her hair.

He stands at the door. She stands at the fireplace. She says, half-
laughing, half-angry, "How can we go out? You have to study, I have
to cook."

He wants at least then to wipe back the sweat, take away the smear,
tuck the straying hair back into place. But these things can't be done
with people around, apt to come in at any moment; proprieties have to
be observed. (This too does not need saying.) Instead he blows the logs

into a proper blaze for her and goes out on to the front verandah with his book.

A while later (he can't tell how long, he's been trying so hard to concentrate) he sees her coming down the path between the trees. She is wearing her green going-out sari and the jasmine in her hair; she smiles at him as she goes past, and enters the house. After that he is able to make sense of what he is reading.

At the end of the chapter, he puts the the book down and goes into the kitchen to say, "Thank goodness you did manage to get out for a walk." She says, bewildered: "What?" And he sees the sweat still streaming down her face, and the same smear of soot across her forehead.

The notion of an astral body (*sukshma sharira*, or subtle body, in the precise Sanskrit), among so many other inheritances, is a commonplace in the clan—it's just there, though not necessarily for everyday use; like furniture in the attic. (Except we have no attics and generally less furniture to store.) But he is old and honest, acknowledging all of this with one hand and trying to explain her quality with the other.

"I *saw* her, I tell you. That's all I know. I may have made it up from wanting it so much. She always knew what I wanted, without my having to tell her, and I always knew what she—"

This time, when he stops, it is not because he can't put it into words. Unnoticed by us, others have come in to listen: a son-in-law here, a daughter there, a cousin somewhere else, a grandniece on the steps.

In their presence he will not speak.

And in his absence they will.

At least, those relatives on the outer fringes, not those in the house. I walk home from school one day to find them visiting, discussing like some misplaced Greek chorus the extraordinary closeness between the two of us.

"Ever since you were a baby," one says. "You always screamed in fright at strangers, but the first time you saw your grandfather, that time he came to visit you all in Cuddappah, you climbed on his lap right away and wouldn't get off." I also, it turns out, at age three, went staggering over to his second wife with a mammoth, long-handled broomstick generally used to sweep cobwebs off ceilings, and told her to GET OUT.

Behind their eyes they chew ruminatively over thoughts of reincarnation, and all of a sudden it makes me angry; for while I admit the rest of the furniture in the attic, I also know quite simply that now I can't abide the woman only because she has hurt my mother, and I'm fierce about that.

It doesn't stop there. The old man talks to me, they say (pushing the point), not only because I am safely a child but because I remind him of his first wife.

"*Me?*" Incredulous, I see myself: ineptly blundering into my teens, schoolbooks under one arm and ankle bells from dancing class slung over the other. "I've seen the old family photographs, she's not like me at all. Not a bit."

"A way you have is a way she had."

There, in the scope of that incongruity, it breaks in upon me: the scope of his daily starvation for her. And the pain for the second wife as well, having to live up to a dead paragon, especially when all is so restrained that nothing can surface.

Is that why she acts as she does? Does it stay with her . . . being reduced to a cobweb by even a three-year-old? Is she hurt enough, *seeing* enough, to recognize any of this? If she did, would that make any difference? (. . . is comprehended pain any different from blind pain, no matter what the books say? is the common bread of jealousy any

191

better? . . .) Has she tried so unsuccessfully to be a partner that she must boss him and take it out on his first wife's children—or has she tried at all? Does she care for him or is she just stuck with him?

How easy for those in this room who have recourse to the attic to explain it all away by reincarnation, dismiss her predicament and that of her victims by saying she is not an old soul and needs another few lifetimes to work out her salvation. Does that in any way lessen her pain or alleviate her actions?

To me, this part of the attic is rather like not being able to see the trees for the woods. I can't reach for it unless I'm allowed to understand precisely what each piece of furniture is made of, at the time I am looking at it. Yes, she is forgiven by those she abused. In time, with the genuine kinship and affection among brothers and sisters and cousins, the whole notion of "step-hood" will become irrelevant, even outmoded, a passing anomaly. And I will never really know—here it comes again—whether the pain I attribute to her is the pain *she* feels:

Investitures. Will we ever get away from investitures—of emotion, responsibility, all the rest? But I am like the old man: though it is crying out in me, I have no words for this. They have to be not just clothed but born, later, their alphabet reconstructed slowly out of living.

At the time I just stand there, scratching the toe of one foot against the heel of the other, and suddenly it is too much. I can't take it all in. Moments. Not only of conception and circumstance, but decision, lenience, mistake. The moments that make generations. The smallness and enormity of it. . . .

Their life in that house overtakes me. And other lives in other houses and non-houses. And I am stupidly afraid I shall start to weep and not be able to stop, and the visitors will exchange glances and say, "It's that *age*, you know," and I won't give them that satisfaction.

So I don't cry. I ponder over it and ponder over it, and at last when I am grown and he is dead, and there is a generation that has forgotten and a generation that doesn't know, I begin to glimpse how it might have come to pass, how it might have been, for him, for each of them. And there is no way now, no way at all, to verify my perceptions.

Yet something else undeniably stays with me and with the rest of us— perhaps in what is called the fullness of time, which does not diminish its losses.

During Grandfather's last illness, his children and grandchildren gather in the house. Some take days to arrive from the north or north-west or northeast. Everyone sleeps on mats ranged in rows along the floor. One granddaughter, who must be specially tended, has suffered a miscarriage; another (myself) gets a scholarship to study abroad; a grandson starts a new job; a cousin wants to renounce his, preferring the ascetic life. Some of the women sit out on the verandah, talking together and companionably sorting tamarinds to be preserved until the next season. And it is as if he gives us leave to do it all. There's no feeling of unfitness or outrage now, only a yielding of place, a time for living and a time for dying. How exactly he is able to set them side by side, I am never to know either. "Happy" endings don't tell you. But his death somehow manages to accommodate life, even the breakages of his own; and in the end he leaves behind a sense not of cessation but of continuity.

Epilogue

How difficult to do this: to demand a particular and different space for a certain literature of perception.

To abjure standard derivatives for a sustained inner syntax. To speak with only a lived right, and no claims of authority whatever—no easily recognizable slots to be fitted into, or any sanctioned platforms to stand on—no reliance placed upon either the surveys of research, or the safeties of scholarship, or the props of fiction.

When the only touchstone lies in living and nothing else, of course there are pitfalls everywhere.

Human fallibility for a basic. Being mistaken, to begin with. The danger of sounding didactic when you abandon indirect speech (of "characters," "viewpoints," or, except once, the leavening of a "story.")

The danger of insights taking on the aspect of generalizations: something that may be evaded in narrative, behind the chosen voice, and avoided in areas of specialized knowledge—academic or otherwise—whose bets can be hedged and statements protected professionally, with innumerable conditional clauses. Not here.

This must distill something that doesn't ride on dailiness, let alone gathered data, but evolves afresh from it . . . stripping away both the explicit dailiness of a diary and the implicit dailiness of a familiarity that is necessary as a background if fiction is to convince. Where the materials may be autobiographical, but the concerns are not.

And these concerns have to inhabit their own spaces, build their innate scaffolding, rejecting any credentials created by strategies of argument for the playing out of a paradox or a theme or an answer.

I have no "answers." How can I, when I'm always telling me: "Don't be a borrower of other people's definitions. Quarrel with yourself first, to test your truth. And then, maybe, it will elect its form."

When you set out to do what seems impossible, you struggle against its possible futility; and yet you cannot in a way know something until you have lived the limits of it, in both senses of the word.

No, I can't answer at all, just hope—fitfully—to illuminate . . . and focus. Widening and narrowing, widening and narrowing, the human lens; meanwhile knowing in my own cells how sometimes a sense of perspective can be deadly to the sense of a single purpose. (Especially at those points of living and dying when language and art and thought can become an intrusion.)

—All the losses when this inner goal can't be put first; all the gains. Sifting themselves out and through the humanity of us all.

Acknowledgments

Parts of this book have appeared in different format and title in *The Iowa Review, Horizon, Parabola, River Styx,* and *Frontiers* (the feminist journal of the University of Colorado). A segment of "Line in the Dark" was included in a collection of contemporary women's writing, *Extended Outlooks,* edited by Jane Cooper, Gwen Head, Adelaide Morris, and Marcia Southwick (New York: Macmillan, 1983). The first part of "Bitter Gourd and Green Mango" appeared in *The Helicon Nine Reader: A Celebration of Women in the Arts,* edited by Gloria Vando Hickok (Kansas City: Helicon Nine Editions, 1990), and in my collected fiction, *Birthday Deathday* (London: Women's Press, 1985, and New Delhi: Penguin India, 1992). "Dance Story" was published in French translation as "Professeur de Danse" by *Initiations* (Brussells, 1996).

Thanks to Linda Norton, my editor, for her faith in this book; to Dore Brown for her unfailing help; to Leslie Larson for her thoughtfulness; and to designer Nola Burger for her clarity of eye and mind.

I am grateful to the MacDowell Colony, Peterborough, NH; the Corporation of Yaddo, NY; and the Helene Wurlitzer Foundation of New Mexico, Taos, where portions of this book were written.

Loving thanks to Vrinda Kumble for pointing out the bird in the first place; to Sophia Steriades Morgan for helping me define some of its spaces; and to Sarah Appleton Weber for deeply shared work and permission to quote from her letter.

The space around this book is blessed with friendships that have helped it to happen—above all the sensitivity and support of Fleur Weymouth, perfect reader and critic. She and Louise Baum have been godmothers to the manuscript in more ways than one, arranging for secretarial assistance when I was most in need of it. Nicole Newman's lovely glowing presence not only provided that assistance but made a success of hanging my solo art show as well. Kay Flavell's encouragement rescued the book from the back of a desk drawer; Marguerite Bouvard and Kitty Byrnes Liebhardt answered a last-minute SOS. A toast also to the following: Dorothy Kethler, Susan Unterberg, Liz Sparks, Jane Cooper, Jeriann Hilderley, Phyllis Kenevan, Rita Sutcliffe, and to Leela Kasturi with admiration and conversations going a long long way back. An appreciation of other old friends is also in order here: Nancy Willard and Eric Lindbloom; Jim Kimble for the times we walked together to the end of a thought; Sofie Lardas; and the cherished memory of poet and translator Konstantinos Lardas.

I could not have survived some of these past few years without Peter S. Beagle and my brother, Arun Hejmadi. Sumana Chandavarkar, my sister, sent lifelines of advice across continents. As for my mother, Rukma Hejmadi: words quite simply come to a stop.

Bibliography

I owe a special debt to two books from India that have proved invaluable in verifying facts on Indian jewelry:

Brijbhushan, Jamila. *Indian Jewellery, Ornaments and Decorative Design.* First edition. Bombay: DB Taraporevala & Sons, 1956.

Dongerkery, Kamala. *Jewellery and Personal Adornment in India.* New Delhi: The Indian Council for Cultural Relations, 1970.

Cooper, Jane. *Green Notebook, Winter Road.* Gardiner, Maine: Tilbury House, 1994.

————. *Scaffolding*. Gardiner, Maine: Tilbury House, 1993.

Osler, Mirabel. *A Gentle Plea for Chaos*. New York: Simon & Schuster, 1989.

Sackville-West, Vita. *Vita Sackville-West's Garden Books*. New York: Atheneum, 1969.

White, Katherine S. *Onward and Upward in the Garden*. New York: Farrar, Straus and Giroux, 1979.

Yanagi, Soetsu. *The Unknown Craftsman*. Revised edition. Tokyo: Kodansha International, 1989.

Designer
Nola Burger

Compositor
Binghamton Valley Composition

Text
11.25/14.75 Fournier

Display
Gill Sans Light and Book

Printer and Binder
Maple Vail